2-minute ENCOURAGERS for teachers

by craig**jutila**

Group

Loveland, Colorado

www.group.com

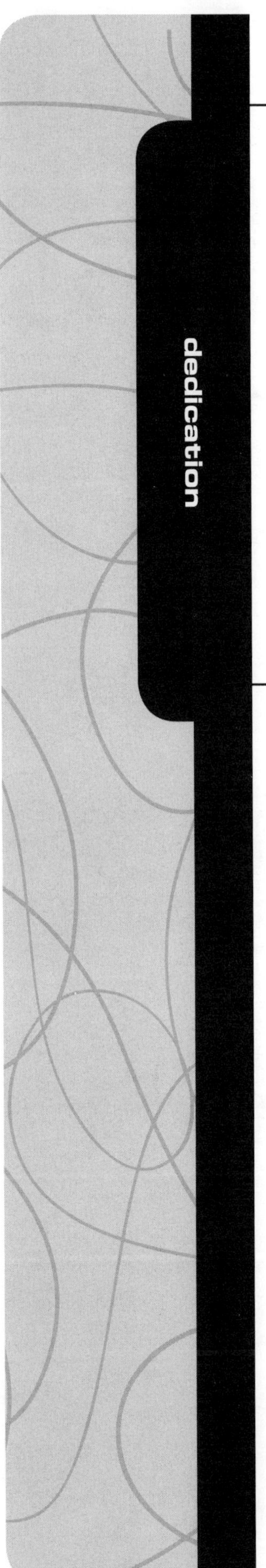

I want to dedicate this book to all of our children's ministry volunteer leaders at Saddleback Church. What a journey we have been on, and yet we've only just begun!

Thank you for your willing sacrifice to love, honor, value, respect, lead, and model for the children you build relationships with each week. Your weekly commitment to lead is unprecedented, and to watch children "line up" to see their favorite leader brings tears to my eyes.

The children are not coming for the curriculum, but for the love that you model for them each week. God bless you for your joyful, serving hearts. You are making a difference in the world! As always, remember, *things are caught, not*...well, you know!

When I think of encouragement, I think of you. I love you all.

2-Minute Encouragers for Teachers

Visit our Web site: **www.group.com**

Credits
Editor: Debbie Gowensmith
Creative Development Editor: Mikal Keefer
Chief Creative Officer: Joani Schultz
Copy Editor: Dena Twinem
Art Director: Jean Bruns
Design and Production: Toolbox Creative
Cover Art Director: Bambi Eitel
Cover Designer: Susan Tripp
Production Manager: Peggy Naylor

Library of Congress Cataloging-in-Publication Data
Jutila, Craig, 1965-
2-minute encouragers for teachers / by Craig Jutila.
p. cm.
ISBN 0-7644-2771-7 (pbk. : alk. paper)
1. Sunday school teachers--Prayer-books and devotions--English. I. Title: Two minute encouragers for teachers. II. Title.
BV4596.S9J88 2004
242'.68--dc22 2004018864

10 9 8 7 6 5 4 3 2 1 14 13 12 11 10 09 08 07 06 05

Printed in the United States of America.

table of contents

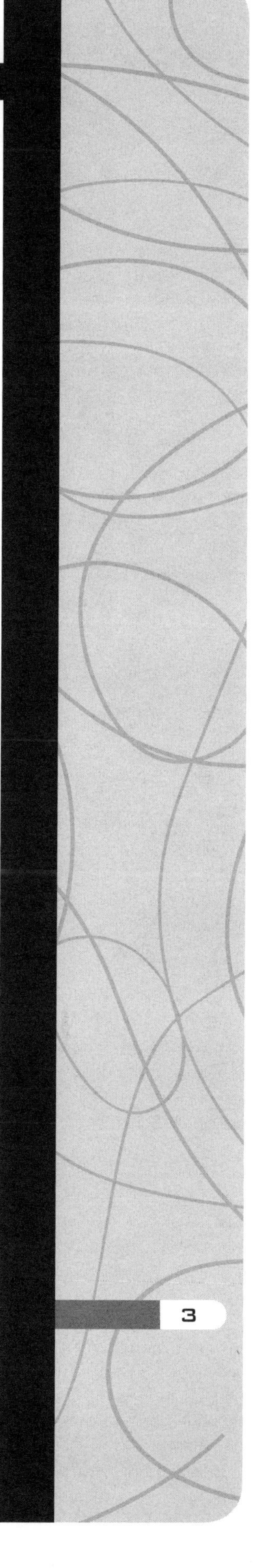

Encouragement is worth its weight in gold.

Give a compliment to most people and they'll perk up all day. If you *really* encourage people, they'll rev up for a solid week.

So why is encouragement so rare in children's ministry? Volunteer teachers often report they're seldom thanked or encouraged for the important work they do.

Here are three reasons it can be tough to encourage teachers...

We're busy.

Sunday morning, when most teachers are in the church building, we're dashing around finding craft supplies. We don't have time to pat every volunteer on the back with an encouraging word.

And getting an evening free to phone all the teachers? *That's* not going to happen.

So we let weeks slide into months—without ever directly contacting volunteers to encourage them in their service to kids.

We aren't sure what to say.

After you've said, "Thanks for making a difference," what's next?

Teachers tell us that recognition is fine, but they *also* want to grow in their own relationships with God. And they want friendship-building opportunities to connect with other teachers. *That's* what encourages teachers most.

But how can you deliver it?

We seldom receive encouragement ourselves.

Good news—using the fifty-two already-prepared teacher encouragements you'll find in this book will prompt rave reviews from your teachers...and that's encouragement directed back to *you.*

When you start a culture of encouragement, you benefit too. You'll find your teachers enjoy teaching more...are generous in their affirmation of you...are quicker to recruit their friends to join your teaching team...and stick longer as volunteers!

When encouragement can do all that for your teachers and your children's ministry, why wait another minute to get started?

This book makes it easy to encourage teachers—all year long!

2-Minute Encouragers for Teachers is a complete *year* of weekly, encouraging connections with every teacher in your church.

Each week you'll...

- **encourage** teachers with a fun story that highlights an encouraging topic,
- **engage** teachers by suggesting a way they can encourage others,
- **empower** teachers by sharing a relevant Scripture passage, and
- **equip** teachers as they answer questions that lead to life application. Plus, your teachers will...
- **experience** life-changing, reflective prayer that leads to growth.

Photocopy the weekly encouragers printed here to give to your teachers, or import the text into your own newsletters. Tweak the material so it fits your staff and situation perfectly. Add your own flourishes. These encouragers are yours to use as you like with your church staff!

And make it an even *cooler* experience by burning copies of the audio CD that features Craig Jutila sharing the encouraging stories you'll find in this book! Make as many copies of the CD as you'd like for your local church use.

Craig has shared these same stories with his own staff and seen firsthand how they've touched and fired up teachers at Saddleback Community Church.

Don't let encouragement be a random thing with your teachers—deliver it weekly with *2-Minute Encouragers for Teachers*!

And here's a bonus for you...

Starting on page 110, you'll find photocopiable "encouragement posters" to tack up on a bulletin board or slide into your teachers' in-boxes. These posters feature words from the most powerful source of encouragement of all: God's Word.

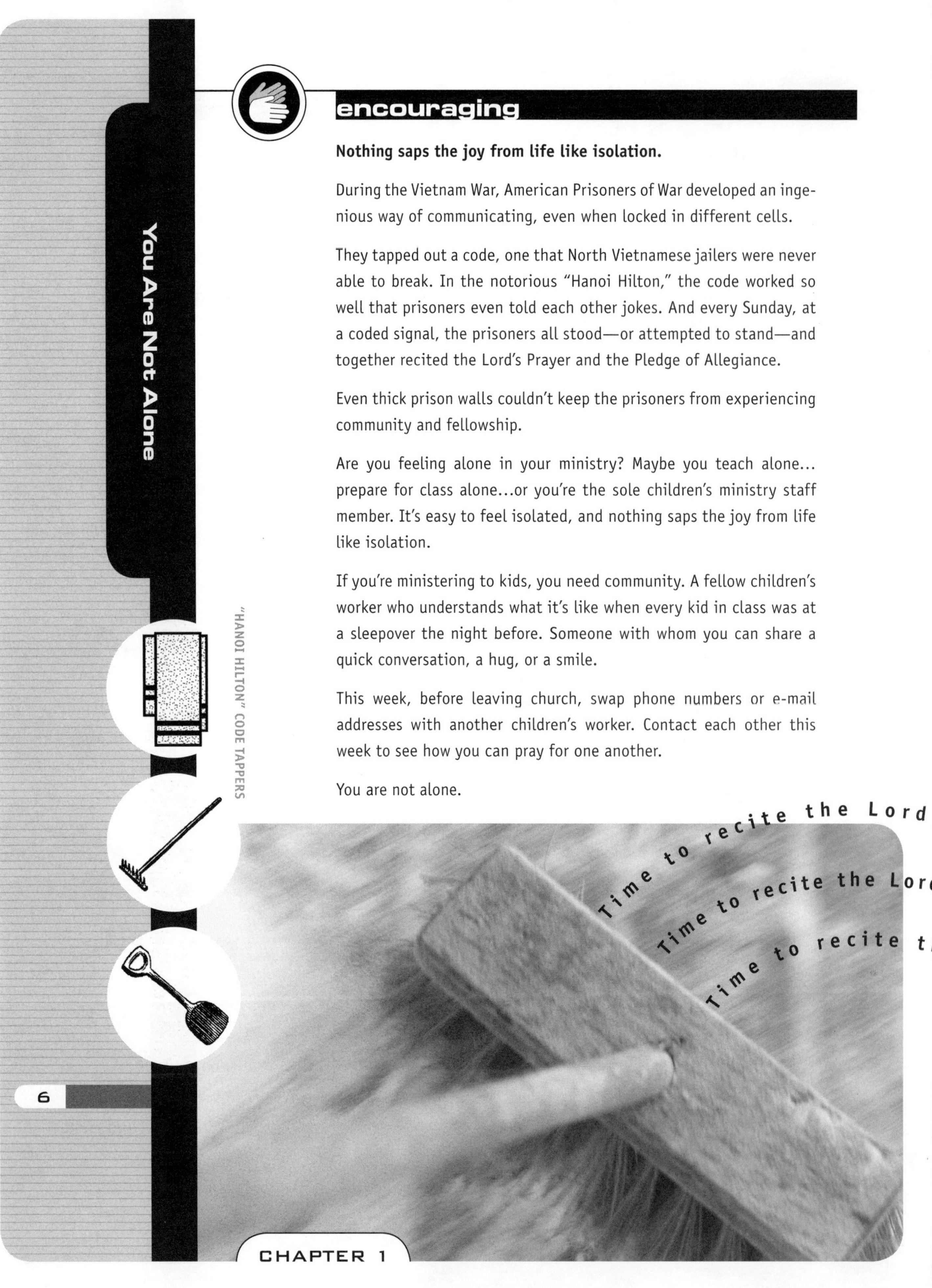

encouraging

Nothing saps the joy from life like isolation.

During the Vietnam War, American Prisoners of War developed an ingenious way of communicating, even when locked in different cells.

They tapped out a code, one that North Vietnamese jailers were never able to break. In the notorious "Hanoi Hilton," the code worked so well that prisoners even told each other jokes. And every Sunday, at a coded signal, the prisoners all stood—or attempted to stand—and together recited the Lord's Prayer and the Pledge of Allegiance.

Even thick prison walls couldn't keep the prisoners from experiencing community and fellowship.

Are you feeling alone in your ministry? Maybe you teach alone... prepare for class alone...or you're the sole children's ministry staff member. It's easy to feel isolated, and nothing saps the joy from life like isolation.

If you're ministering to kids, you need community. A fellow children's worker who understands what it's like when every kid in class was at a sleepover the night before. Someone with whom you can share a quick conversation, a hug, or a smile.

This week, before leaving church, swap phone numbers or e-mail addresses with another children's worker. Contact each other this week to see how you can pray for one another.

You are not alone.

engaging

You're not alone in ministry.

This week, before leaving church, swap phone numbers or e-mail addresses with another children's worker. Touch base this week to see how you can pray for one another.

empowering

"Let us think about each other and help each other to show love and do good deeds. You should not stay away from the church meetings, as some are doing, but you should meet together and encourage each other. Do this even more as you see the day coming."

—Hebrews 10:24-25 *(New Century Version)*

equipping

As we lead children, we want to reflect the love of Christ. That becomes increasingly difficult if we're feeling isolated or alone.

- Who are people who offer you encouragement or affirmation as you serve children?

- What are the obstacles and walls in your life that separate you from others?

- What would help you overcome those obstacles and walls? What might it require from you? from others?

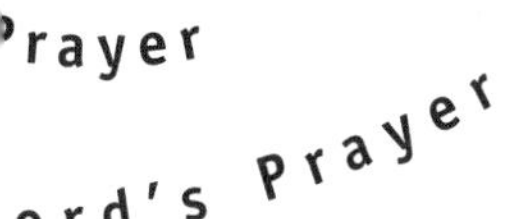

experiencing

Meditate and pray this week about isolation in your life and ministry...

Lord, help me see the walls and obstacles in my life that separate me from you and your people. You saw how walls separate people during your ministry on earth, Jesus. You saw walls that separated Jew from Samaritan, men from women, the rich from the poor, and you reached across those walls. You dismantled them. Guide me in dismantling walls that separate me from others, God, so I can serve others in your name. Amen.

encouraging

It's been listed as one of the most deadly train accidents ever. On March 2, 1944, train 8017 pulled out of its station in Italy. Not long after, almost all of its passengers—more than five hundred people—were dead.

The train didn't jump the tracks or explode or crash. In fact, the train suffered no external damage at all.

So why did so many people die?

As the train pulled into a long tunnel, it apparently began to lose traction. There in the dark tunnel, faced with the unknown, the engineers had to react to an unclear situation. Precisely what they did, no one knows for sure. But we do know they lacked the clarity to exit the tunnel quickly. Carbon monoxide fumes from the low-grade coal spewing out of the train's smokestack poisoned more than five hundred people.

Clarity empowers you to act decisively—and fast. So instead of being stuck in a dark, potentially dangerous situation, debating what to do, you'll already know.

Take time *now* to review classroom policies. Be sure you're clear about your ministry's purpose or mission and about the nuts and bolts of your ministry role. Clarity counts—so be sure you've done your homework. If your ministry's policies aren't yet on paper, volunteer to make that happen.

Clarity helps everyone on your team be on the same page and keeps everyone working together.

Is your head clear?

engaging

When you're clear about the mission and purpose of your children's ministry, and about policies and procedures, many decisions are easy to make because they're *already* made.

Review your ministry's handbook this week. If there's anything you don't understand, call your ministry leader to get clarification. Take the initiative to get the information you need.

empowering

"Then make me truly happy by agreeing wholeheartedly with each other, loving one another, and working together with one heart and purpose." —Philippians 2:2 *(New Living Translation)*

equipping

Confusion breeds frustration, but clarity breeds confidence.

- In what ways does being clear about your role affect your response to a task?
- In what areas of your ministry do you feel clear, comfortable, and confident?
- In what areas could you use clarification? Who might give it to you? How will you ask?

experiencing

Meditate and pray this week about areas in your life and ministry in which you need clarification...

Lord, thank you for the opportunity to serve. When I feel stuck and don't know what to do, help me remember that there are people who'll help clarify my role. When I feel frustrated, help me remember I'm empowered to act. Guide me, God, so I can glorify you in all my actions and relationships. Amen.

encouraging

If we don't communicate with each other, we're fighting a losing battle.

Case in point: In 1991, U.S. military leaders created a campaign to roust the invading Iraqi army from the tiny nation of Kuwait. On January 17, the United States launched Operation Desert Storm with air assaults on strategic Iraqi targets. Which targets do you think were among the first?

You might expect the United States to first seek and destroy Iraqi tanks or airplanes. Instead, the U.S. military took out Iraq's radar and communication infrastructure. Without a way to communicate and plan together, the Iraqi leadership soon lost control over its forces.

You can probably envision the loss of control that occurs when communication breaks down between teachers!

You are an essential member of a teaching fellowship. Being a part of this fellowship means spending time talking with one another. This week, be sure to call each of your co-leaders. Set up a schedule to regularly communicate with each other so everyone is informed and has a chance to share. It will take you just a few minutes to be sure you're on the same page as your fellow servants!

If we don't **communicate** with each other, we're fighting a **losing battle.**

engaging

This week, call your co-teachers. Arrange a time to regularly communicate with each other. Nothing is more encouraging than knowing your input is valued and that you're in the information loop!

empowering

"An unreliable messenger can cause a lot of trouble. Reliable communication permits progress." —Proverbs 13:17 *(The Living Bible)*

equipping

You are part of a team, and communication is an important key to your team's ministry success. Communication permits progress.

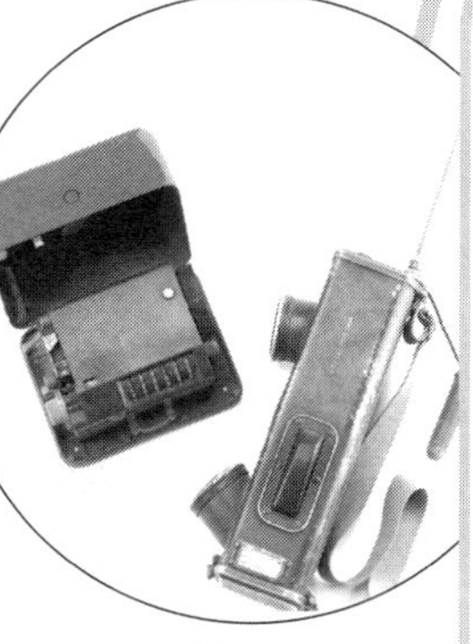

- What prevents you from opening lines of communication with others?

- How have you been encouraged through someone's words?

- How can you communicate encouragement to others?

experiencing

Meditate and pray this week about communicating with others...

Lord, thank you for the blessing of communicating with you through prayer. It's wonderful to be able to talk with you. I sometimes forget how important communication is—especially during the hectic race of everyday life. Help me to remember to be still so I can communicate with others...and with you. Amen.

encouraging

I recently was driving down the Pennsylvania Turnpike when I came across a work crew improving the road. I was running late, I was in unfamiliar territory, and as traffic slowed I thought, *These people are making me late. Why didn't they plan the roadwork for the evening hours?* My attention was divided between watching the road, talking on my cell phone to get directions, and looking at a map.

The traffic slowed further, and my irritation ratcheted up another notch. Suddenly a bright orange road sign caught my attention. It read, "Please slow down. My daddy works here." Another sign read, "Please slow down. My mommy works here."

My frustration evaporated. I hung up the phone, put down the map, and focused on the people working around me. Why? Because children's parents were working there.

Usually the road signs read, "Slow down. Men at work." That sign relays a fact. The other signs, a powerfully emotive word picture. It was those signs that changed my behavior.

As teachers, we need to communicate in an equally powerful way if we want to change lives.

Spend a few extra minutes this week studying the lesson or Scripture you'll share with children. With what word pictures and emotions can you communicate the powerful truth *behind* the facts?

engaging

Spend a few extra minutes this week studying the lesson or Scripture you'll share with children. What word pictures and emotions can you share that will powerfully communicate the truth *behind* the facts?

empowering

"Be pleasant and hold their interest when you speak the message. Choose your words carefully and be ready to give answers to anyone who asks questions."

—Colossians 4:6 *(Contemporary English Version)*

equipping

We're about life change, not just pumping kids full of information. As we find ways to encourage kids to have a relationship with God and we fill our lessons with discovery, we involve more than kids' heads—we involve their hearts.

- What discoveries or experiences have moved you to change your life?

- How would you describe the impact of the gospel on your life?

- How can you share with your kids the power of that impact?

experiencing

Meditate and pray this week about the power of life-changing communication...

Lord, please help me communicate truth to the children in my care and encourage them to have a relationship with you. Work through me, God, to help learners love and follow you. And thank you, Lord, for the privilege and honor of participating in your life-changing work. Amen.

encouraging

You're an employee in one of the last textile factories in New England. The factory in which you and three thousand other workers labor has just been destroyed by a fire. Your seventy-seven-year-old employer *could* collect the $300 million insurance check and retire, leaving you jobless.

But instead, Aaron Feuerstein, owner of the ninety-year-old Malden Mills textile factory, shocked the nation when he announced he'd rebuild. Even more shocking was his decision to continue paying employees their full salaries for sixty days—at a cost of $25 million.

Said Feuerstein: "It was the right thing to do."

As Feuerstein's employee, you'd thank God your leader believes in providing for you through thick and thin.

As you work with children, you provide for *them* through thick and thin too. You spend yourself when you feel great and when you feel tired, when they're little angels and when they're less than perfect.

Feuerstein's values sustained and directed him during his business crisis. What are the values that sustain and direct you and bring you back to serve children week after week? Write them down, and place the list in your Bible where you'll see them on days when it feels like rebuilding is just too much work.

engaging

Your true values emerge when there's a crisis. Think about the values that sustain you when *you* face difficulties as a teacher. What is it that brings you back to serve children week after week? Write down those values, and place them in your Bible where you'll see them during tough times.

empowering

"I know how to live in poverty or prosperity. No matter what the situation, I've learned the secret of how to live when I'm full or when I'm hungry, when I have too much or when I have too little. I can do everything through Christ who strengthens me."

—Philippians 4:12-13 *(God's Word)*

equipping

Remember: We make a living by what we get. We make a life by what we give.

- What does it mean to you to be able to provide for children through teaching?
- What values sustain you through thick and thin?
- How can you ask others to provide support and encouragement for you when you're experiencing tough times?

experiencing

Meditate and pray this week about a faithful life that consistently provides...

Lord, thank you for providing everything I need to get through life. Thank you for being with me all the time, for carrying me when times get tough. Help me, God, to seek you when I'm struggling and to be sensitive and willing to help when others are struggling. Amen.

encouraging

Have you ever seen a flock of geese flying overhead? I'm always astounded by the precision of their formation, each bird slightly behind, above, and to the side of the bird in front.

Flying in this "V" formation isn't a coincidence. Each bird is reducing the wind resistance for the next bird. Working together, the geese can fly for much greater distances. The geese also can see each other better, as if they're looking out for one another.

When the lead goose gets tired, it falls back and allows another goose to take the lead. When a goose falls out of formation, it immediately feels the drag of unblocked wind resistance.

You're part of such a "flock." You don't have to fly alone because your colleagues are there to ease your burdens and look out for you. Pray with and for another children's worker this week. And let that flock member pray for you.

engaging

Take a moment before or after class to share prayer requests with each other. Then, as a flock, stand in a circle, hold hands, and take turns praying for the person on the right. Ask God to bless one another's lives.

empowering

"Be sure that you live in a way that brings honor to the Good News of Christ. Then whether I come and visit you or am away from you, I will hear good things about you. I will hear that you continue strong with one purpose and that you work together as a team for the faith of the Good News."

—Philippians 1:27 *(International Children's Bible)*

equipping

A flock of geese flying in formation can teach us a great deal about the value of vulnerability and teamwork.

- How does the example of geese remind you of your team at church? What does the example of your team teach you?
- How do you allow others to assist you when you're wounded or tired? How can you help other children's workers on your team rest?
- How does it make you feel to know that, rather than being alone, your flock is working together?

experiencing

Meditate and pray this week about togetherness and teamwork in your life and ministry...

Lord, sometimes I feel like I'm flying directly into a headwind. Help me to remember that with your strength, I can soar on wings like eagles. Help me to remember that I'm not alone, that I have friends and colleagues who can help me go the distance. Thank you for togetherness. Amen.

encouraging

How important is it to be prepared when you work with kids?

We'd probably all vote that it's very important—critical even—but our actions might tell another story. There's a joke that's made the rounds for years that makes a good point about being prepared. Here's the version I heard most recently:

A man named Tony was raised in Rome, but moved to New York when he was a teenager. In time he married, and when his son was ten, Tony took the boy to Rome to show the lad Daddy's old neighborhood.

As they walked down the street, Tony pointed out a shoe repair shop. "When we were young, we didn't buy new shoes every year," he said. "We were poor, so we had old Pino there fix our shoes. In fact, I went there so often he might remember me if the old guy's still alive."

The man and his son walked into the dark, tiny shop where shoes filled cubicles from the floor to the ceiling. It had been twenty years, but Pino—an elderly man with a worn face—flashed a smile. "Ah, little Tony!" he cried. The two men embraced, Tony introduced his boy, and Tony shook his head in amazement.

"I didn't really think you'd remember me," Tony said.

"I never forget a customer," Pino bragged, puffing out his chest. "I'm prepared when my customers walk through the door."

"I'm not sure you could still call me a customer," Tony said. "I haven't been in here since I moved away twenty years ago."

"Ah, but before you left, you brought in a pair of brown leather shoes to mend," Pino said.

Tony slapped his forehead. "That's right! Unbelievable! I forgot to pick them up."

"You see how prepared Pino is?" the old man said, wagging a finger. "I know your name. I know what shoes you brought in."

"Amazing," Tony admitted. "And embarrassing. You've been ready for me to walk back in for twenty years, and I totally forgot. Let me at least take care of the bill. How much do I owe you?

"I'm not sure," Pino said with a shrug. "I haven't fixed the shoes yet. Come back next Friday."

So much for Pino being prepared for his customers. He knew *what* to do, and who to do it *for,* but he never got around to actually doing the job.

Not repairing a pair of shoes is one thing. Not preparing to share God's Word with kids—that's something else. It's critical we prepare spiritually for the kids and parents we minister to each week.

engaging

This next week, spend an hour looking through, praying through, and planning through your lesson. Even if you won't be up front teaching the lesson, preparation will boost your confidence so you can focus on the children.

empowering

"Always be ready to defend your confidence [in God] when anyone asks you to explain it. However, make your defense with gentleness and respect."—1 Peter 3:15b *(God's Word)*

equipping

The importance of being prepared cannot be overstated. A good start almost always leads to a good finish.

- When has solid preparation paid off for you?
- What do you need to do in order to feel well-prepared for teaching?
- How can others help you to feel better prepared? How can you help others?

experiencing

Meditate and pray this week about preparation in your life and ministry...

Lord, it can be difficult to make the time to prepare well for teaching—even though I know it's important to do so. Please open up spaces in my day and my week, and help me to recognize opportunities to prepare. Help me to prepare effectively so I can be ready to serve. Thank you, Lord. Amen.

encouraging

Ever heard of Saint Louis University? Probably not, yet the school made a major contribution to the world of collegiate sports.

In the early 1900s, the game of football was receiving flak—even from President Theodore Roosevelt—because of the game's violence. Officials hoped that a simple rule change allowing the forward pass would make the game safer.

Universities were slow to adapt. But coach Eddie Cochems of Saint Louis University made history by calling the first forward pass play in 1906. Though that first attempt was incomplete, Saint Louis went on to an undefeated season in which they outscored opponents 407 to 11! Other schools realized that if they wanted to win, they'd have to adapt too.

Adapting is one of the most difficult things to do in life. As coach Cochems knew, adaptation carries risk. Could he have failed? Sure. Was it easy? Not likely, especially after the first attempt failed. But the team was determined to make the change and reap the benefits.

How open is your team to making needed changes to improve your ministry program? How open are *you?*

engaging

It's easier to adapt and make changes when the team is behind those changes. This week, agree with other teachers to follow through on a change you've been aching to make. Together, write down the change you've all decided to make, and have everyone sign his or her name to it. Agree to evaluate the change after a reasonable amount of time to make sure you've made a change for the better.

empowering

"Without good direction, people lose their way; the more wise counsel you follow, the better your chances."

—Proverbs 11:14 *(The Message)*

equipping

Here are three questions worth answering when it comes to being adaptable and open to changes.

- What—or who—has helped you ease into changes you've been encouraged to make in the past?
- What do you need to change in your life to grow stronger spiritually?
- What can you change or adapt to be more effective in serving children?

experiencing

Meditate and pray this week about adaptation and change in your life and ministry...

Lord, change can be scary. Like Jesus' disciples on a stormy sea, I desire the security of what is known. Change brings risk, and risk brings anxiety and fear. But change also generates growth. Help me to wisely seek and embrace necessary changes. Help me to face the risks, to adapt despite the possibilities for failure. Help me learn from the experience, resting in the confidence that you can create good out of any situation. Thank you, God, for guiding me through the stormy seas of change. Amen.

encouraging

What do you do when life throws you a lemon? Make lemonade! What do you do when wind blows sand from your beach towel into your face? Make a weighted beach towel!

At least that's what Joanne Marlow did.

The struggling businesswoman headed to the beach for a well-deserved break. She applied suntan oil and prepared to relax. Just then, a gust of wind lifted her towel and covered her in sand. A friend suggested that Joanne channel her frustration into an opportunity.

Joanne Marlow's weighted beach towels hit the market eight weeks later, and her company earned $4.5 million its first year.

As you serve in ministry, you'll take an occasional faceful of sand—if not today, then someday soon. But you've faced challenges before and survived.

Today, shift your vocabulary from "This is a *big problem*" to "This is a *huge opportunity!*" Repeat this sentence whenever you face challenges: "This situation presents a *wonderful* opportunity!"

engaging

Today, decide to shift your vocabulary from "This is a *big problem*" to "This is a *huge opportunity!*" Repeat this sentence out loud. Now repeat it again...and again. Let the words sink into your heart and attitude.

empowering

"Dear brothers and sisters, whenever trouble comes your way, let it be an opportunity for joy."—James 1:2 *(NLT)*

equipping

The way we react to circumstances in our lives depends so much on how we frame what we're facing. The pessimist may be considered more practical, but a pessimist wouldn't have invented the weighted beach towel!

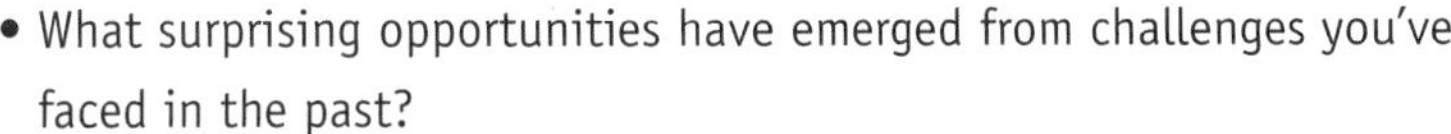

- What surprising opportunities have emerged from challenges you've faced in the past?

- What challenges are you facing today?

- What opportunities are hidden within those challenges?

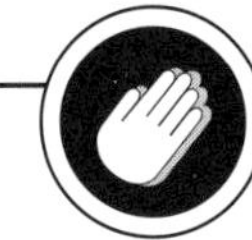

experiencing

Meditate and pray this week about opportunities in your life and ministry...

Lord, when "sand hits me in the face," I often wish I could close my eyes and ignore the pain. But you've promised that these challenges truly are opportunities for joy. Thank you for resilience. Thank you for persistence. Thank you for the people around me who help me to see opportunities where I might see only problems. Thank you, God, for your help and strength. Amen.

encouraging

Lou Holtz is a wildly successful college football coach whose enthusiasm seems to permeate his entire staff. He's able to motivate his teams so they perform with excellence. But how?

In the coach's words: "Motivation is simple. You eliminate those who are not motivated."

You may think it's a bit harsh of the coach to "eliminate" those people on his team who aren't enthusiastic about what they do. But the Bible also sets the bar high on enthusiasm. It says we should work as if we're serving the Lord.

Enthusiasm is a choice each of us must make every day. It starts in your mind as you choose to enjoy life and to enjoy serving the Lord. Then it moves to your heart, where it takes the form of passion and energy. People actually can see a change in your life. Your enthusiasm impacts and inspires others, and suddenly you're making a difference in the world.

A couple of questions for you: Are you fired up? enthusiastic? In what ways does it show in how you work with kids in your ministry?

engaging

Are you fired up? enthusiastic? Does it show in how you work with kids? Write down three ways you can embrace enthusiasm and make a difference in the lives of others.

empowering

"Do your work with enthusiasm. Work as if you were serving the Lord, not as if you were serving only men and women."

—Ephesians 6:7 *(NCV)*

equipping

Enthusiasm transforms an average performer into a great performer, an average teacher into a great teacher, and an average student into a great student.

- What in your life fires you up with energy and enthusiasm?
- Who or what helps you to feel enthusiastic about serving the Lord?
- How can you inspire those who may be feeling more apathetic than enthusiastic?

experiencing

Meditate and pray this week about enthusiasm in your life and ministry...

Lord, this world so desperately needs people who are excited about you. Start right here, with me. Renew my heart for you. Infuse in me a tireless enthusiasm for sharing your wonderful blessings with others. Thank you, Lord. Amen.

encouraging

Some people seem to think that fun doesn't belong in church. But church isn't necessarily always supposed to be serious and quiet.

Just how important *is* fun?

Annette Simmons relates a story told by Marti Smye about her father's commitment to fun. When Marti was a child, she and her brother were forced to practice piano daily, despite their dislike for it. Marti's brother even wore a football helmet during piano practice to get across his message.

One day, Marti's brother came running into the kitchen, shouting, "Mom, come look!" Marti, her mother, and her brother ran to the backyard, where the piano was engulfed in flames. Marti's father stood by, calmly watching. He said, "I want my children to know that if it ain't fun, don't do it."

While Marti's father may have been a bit extreme in his devotion to fun, creating a fun learning environment will inspire you...and your kids. Remember to make your room, relationships, and responsibilities fun!

engaging

Gather with a few of your fellow teachers. Take turns sharing words that are synonymous with the word *fun*. Choose one word as the key word for the day. When you see each other at church, repeat the word as a reminder to invite fun into your classrooms, and into your lives.

empowering

"Always be full of joy in the Lord. I say it again—rejoice!" —Philippians 4:4 *(NLT)*

equipping

The attitude with which you approach a situation often affects its outcome. See it as a problem, and it is one. See it as an opportunity, and you'll discover it is one. See it as a chance to have fun, and often you'll find a way to make it fun. Decide that it's fun to serve God by working with kids and guess what? It will be!

- What are the top five things in life that you have fun doing?
- How can you create fun in your classroom, relationships, and responsibilities?
- How can you make time to embrace fun with the kids you serve?

experiencing

Meditate and pray this week about fun in your life and ministry...

Lord, it's clear that you have a sense of humor! Thank you, God, for whimsy and for wit. Thank your for the lightness that accompanies laughter. Thank you for sharing your creative, fun nature with us so that we can share it with others. Amen.

encouraging

Picture a concert pianist sitting rigidly on a piano bench. He gently rests his hands on the keyboard. Then, with a resounding chord, he begins to play.

To the audience, that moment—the moment his hands touch the keys—is a moment of great harmony. But in fact, it's a moment of great tension.

Theodore E. Steinway once said, "In one of our concert grand pianos, 243 taut strings exert a pull of forty thousand pounds on an iron frame. It is proof that out of great tension may come great harmony."

For the grand piano, such tension keeps the instrument in tune. For you and me, tension can bring us into tune with God and one another.

You see, dozens of children, along with their parents, come to your programs and then leave again within a space of just a few hours. This is a rather tense scenario.

But you have a mission, vision, and values. You have well-tuned instruments to aid you. You have practiced skill. Your purposeful ministry is a harmonious concerto, sharing God's beauty and love with children. This is harmonious tension at its very best!

If you don't know the mission of your children's ministry and how you fit, ask. Then trust God to use you, and enjoy the music God makes by using you. No matter what tense moments you face, sing a song of trust in God.

engaging

Yes, it can be tense teaching a lesson to a room full of children...or leading music during children's church...or reaching out to kids you don't particularly understand. But God can use that tension to make you ever more effective in ministry! Trust in God, and ask him to give you peace even as you invest your life in kids and their families.

empowering

"For I am convinced that neither death nor life, neither angels nor demons, neither the present nor the future, nor any powers, neither height nor depth, nor anything else in all creation, will be able to separate us from the love of God that is in Christ Jesus our Lord."

—Romans 8:38-39 *(New International Version)*

equipping

Butterflies in your stomach or a sense of anticipation isn't always a bad thing. It's your body's way of being on "high alert." Use that adrenaline and focus, and trust that God will use you in your ministry role.

- When was a time you experienced tension as you were preparing to serve in children's ministry?

- What areas of your ministry create tense feelings within you?

- How can you trust those feelings and ministry areas to God?

experiencing

Meditate and pray this week about tension and harmony in your life and ministry...

Lord, you are always working on me, shaping me, growing me. As you challenge me, I sometimes feel tense and unsure. I want to remember you during those tense times. Help me to remember that as you encourage me to grow, you are creating greater harmony in my life and ministry. Amen.

encouraging

An urban legend demonstrates the power of kindness.

In a story I wish were true, a limo suffers a flat tire. As the limo driver is trying to wrestle a spare tire out of the trunk, a man stops to offer much-needed assistance. The problem is solved, and the helpful man meets the person inside the limo—the rich and famous Donald Trump.

Mr. Trump asks if he can do anything for the man, who replies that his wife would love to receive flowers from Donald Trump.

Soon thereafter, the story goes, flowers are indeed delivered to the man's wife—along with a note indicating that Mr. Trump has paid off the couple's mortgage.

This story was forwarded countless times because it's a feel-good story. In it someone goes above and beyond to show over-the-top, unreasonable kindness. We love to see it—and we love to receive it.

Sometimes our co-leaders, kids, and their parents are just hoping for "flowers," but we can deliver unreasonable, over-the-top, bless-their-socks-off kindness.

Don't settle for changing a flat tire when you can pay off a mortgage!

PAID

engaging

Pause for a minute to answer this question: If you were going to express amazing, over-the-top, outstanding kindness to one of your co-leaders, kids, or parents, what would you do? How would that kindness look?

empowering

"Glory belongs to God, whose power is at work in us. By this power he can do infinitely more than we can ask or imagine."

—Ephesians 3:20 *(God's Word)*

equipping

We love urban legends like the one on page 30 because we want to believe such kindness exists in our world. We long to see it and maybe even receive it.

The good news is that such rich kindness *does* exist—and it's been offered to you!

- How have people shown "unreasonable kindness" to you?

- What's your reaction to the unreasonable kindness Jesus showed from the cross?

- How can you encourage others with your own kindness?

experiencing

Meditate and pray this week about kindness in your life and ministry...

Lord, I thank and praise you for all the kindness you've showered on me. I want others to experience your kindness, too, so help me to transmit your love to everyone around me. Amen.

encouraging

There's an unconfirmed story of a violinist's persistence that is an inspiration.

The story goes that Itzhak Perlman performed the concert of his life in New York City one evening. What made the concert so amazing was not just Perlman's deft skill and evocative tone, but his reaction to difficulty.

It seems that as Perlman played, one of his violin strings broke. Everyone expected him to call for a replacement string. He didn't. He persisted, playing with three strings and altering the piece in his mind to compensate for the missing string.

All of us have experienced discouragement—times in our lives when one string breaks, then another, then another. We must decide whether to keep playing or to give up.

With God's help, you can keep playing! Work with what you've got, and trust God to bless the results.

engaging

This week, strengthen yourself in the Lord. When you feel hopeless and discouraged, stop what you're doing and pray. Allow God's strength to push you beyond quitting and toward persistence.

empowering

"But that's not all. We also brag when we are suffering. We know that suffering creates endurance, endurance creates character, and character creates confidence."

—Romans 5:3-4 *(God's Word)*

equipping

Persistence is the ability to take one step at a time as you travel through discouraging and disappointing times in your life.

- What "strings" in your life have broken lately?
- How have you persisted in the past when you've been discouraged?
- How can you continue "playing" through the difficult times you face today?

experiencing

Meditate and pray this week about persistence in your life and ministry...

Lord, you understand my brokenness, and you weep with me when I'm troubled. My hope is in you, Lord. I trust your love. Help me to persist through discouraging situations so that I can build the character that brings confidence. My hope is in you, Lord. Amen.

encouraging

When my wife and I woke up this morning, we were both freezing. We forgot to turn on the heater last night.

My wife reminded me it was my turn to run down the stairs and fire up the furnace since she'd done it several times in the past. I, however, challenged her to a game to determine who'd be making that chilly trip.

She agreed, and thus began a deadly serious game of Rock, Paper, Scissors.

I lost the first game and tried to negotiate another round. "How about two out of three?" She agreed—and I lost again. Four out of seven? Six out of ten?

I lost *every* game. I didn't realize my wife was such a great Rock, Paper, Scissors player!

Unfortunately, I missed an opportunity this morning. I should have gotten out of bed immediately and turned on the heater. I should have served my wife the way Jesus served his disciples.

Washing feet or turning on the heater. They're both ways to serve.

engaging

Once a day for the next seven days, seek opportunities to serve someone. You can serve at home, at work, even at the grocery store. Serving others is a great way to deepen your spiritual walk and become a little bit more like Jesus.

empowering

"Be devoted to one another in brotherly love. Honor one another above yourselves."

—Romans 12:10 *(NIV)*

equipping

Serving others is more than adding a "to-do" item to your list. You'll find that it's empowering, because you learn that you're necessary to the team—that they simply couldn't do it without you.

And allowing others to serve you reminds you that everyone is important.

- How have you served others in the past? How have you been served?

- How did it feel to serve? to be served?

- How can you serve others this week? How can you be served?

experiencing

Meditate and pray this week about serving others through your life and ministry...

Lord, thank you for the example of Jesus, who served endlessly while he was on earth. Thank you for continuing to watch over me and serve me every day. I want to be like you, Lord. Open my eyes to see opportunities all around me to serve others...and you. Thank you. Amen.

encouraging

Have you ever seen the face of a child when she receives a present she wasn't expecting? Have you ever seen the face of a child when she receives a present she *was* expecting? It's the same face: bright eyes, bubbly smile, slight gasps of oohs and aahs, surprise, astonishment, and amazement.

Children teach us mischief and fun. They teach us to appreciate even the tiniest miracles around us. They refuse to allow complacency. They approach every part of life with wonder.

I don't think Jesus ever wants us to lose that way of engaging the world.

Have you ever lost your sense of wonder and awe? Misplaced your sense of amazement and surprise? Have you drifted into a rut or redundant routine? Many of us have.

The good news is that we're serving children, and children are the best teachers about wonder and awe in the universe. Learn from your kids this week!

Ooooooooh...
Is that for ME?

engaging

Write down ten things in your life that are worth smiling about. Share them with a children's ministry friend, and ask your friend to share ten things with you. Thank God for allowing us to grow older with childlike hearts.

empowering

"Everyone was gripped with great wonder and awe. And they praised God, saying over and over again, 'We have seen amazing things today.' "—Luke 5:26 *(NLT)*

equipping

Jesus spent a lot of time amazing people. The things he did, the things he said, the way he related to his heavenly Father—they all surprised the people around Jesus.

The children you serve are often amazed too. They're still discovering how the world works, and that creates in them a great capacity for wonder.

- What is it that evokes in you a childlike wonder?

- How can you soak up the wonder your kids experience?

- How can you encourage your children—and yourself—to continue appreciating the tiny miracles that occur every day?

experiencing

Meditate and pray this week about wonder and surprise in your life and ministry...

Lord, the sun came up today. Somewhere in the world flowers opened their petals to the dawn, snowflakes cascaded down by the thousands, and I pulled myself out of bed. Thank you for these miracles—these and the countless more that are happening around the world at this very moment. Amen.

encouraging

The Kingston Trio recorded a song by Billy Edd Wheeler that reminds us how important it is to take leaps of faith.

In the song, a tired, dusty, and powerfully thirsty traveler comes upon a water pump in the middle of a desert. He's overjoyed because he's thirsty down to his toenails. A note directs the traveler to a small jar of water but pleads with him not to drink it. "You'll have to prime the pump...Have faith, my friend, there's water down below" reads the note.

The thirsty traveler is tempted to drink the little jar of hot, fetid water—even a stagnant drop is better than nothing. But he doesn't. He pours in the water and starts pumping like a madman. Within moments, gloriously, cool water bubbles out, and the traveler drinks his fill.

Sometimes the blessing comes when we follow directions—no matter how we feel.

Take a leap of faith this week by taking God at his word.

engaging

Take a risk this week by loving someone the way Jesus loves us. By serving someone the way Jesus serves us. By giving to someone the way Jesus gives to us.

Prime the pump for your spiritual growth.

empowering

"I have commanded you, 'Be strong and courageous! Don't tremble or be terrified, because the Lord your God is with you wherever you go.' "—Joshua 1:9 *(God's Word)*

equipping

Once we're comfortable with the ministry in which we're involved, we tend to stagnate. Innovation and reinvention may feel risky, but have faith—if a new idea doesn't work out, you can always move on to the next experiment!

- How do you feel when you try new things?

- What's it like to take a risk and succeed?

- What areas of your ministry could use some refreshing, perhaps risky, changes—some leaps of faith?

experiencing

Meditate and pray this week about faithfully taking risks in your life and ministry...

Lord, I enjoy the comfort of familiarity. I enjoy an assured success based on past successes. But I also know that you want me to try new ideas, new approaches. Help me to focus on bringing glory to you rather than becoming mired in my own need for success. Help me to be strong and courageous in my life and ministry. Amen.

encouraging

Sometimes a good laugh really helps your day—and your heart—feel much better. There's a good reason. Did you know that laughter carries tremendous health benefits? It relieves tension, and it motivates. Laughter interrupts the "fight-or-flight" response that makes your pulse quicken, your breathing grow shallow, and adrenaline rush through your body.

Perpetual stress, on the other hand, traps your body in the fight-or-flight response. Constant stress weakens your immune system, making you more susceptible to illness.

But laughter—laughter is golden. It can strengthen your immune system while it lowers your blood pressure. It tones the muscles of your face and stomach and even expels stale air from your lungs. Laughter is like a mild cardio workout!

Do you need a good laugh this week? How do you plan to get one?

engaging

Keep an inventory this week of how often you laugh. How many times did you laugh out loud at something that thoroughly delighted you? Discover ways to expose your life to more laughter. You'll be healthier for it!

empowering

"Being cheerful keeps you healthy. It is slow death to be gloomy all the time."

—Proverbs 17:22 (*Today's English Version*)

equipping

Laughter is not only good for you physically, but also spiritually. Learning to laugh at the "cream pies you take in the face" expands your capacity for humility and adds dimension to your relationship with God.

- How do you feel after a good time of laughter with friends or family members?
- How can you share humor with people around you? with God?
- What can you do to increase laughter in your life today?

experiencing

Meditate and pray this week about fun and laughter in your life and ministry...

Lord, you constantly amaze me. Somehow, you knew how important it would be for your people to laugh. Thank you for this release from stress. Thank you for this focus on the positive things in life. Thank you for the gift of laughter. Amen.

encouraging

While getting ready for school one day, our six-year-old son, Cameron, told me he'd dropped his toothbrush in the toilet. I responded, "That's super, Cameron. Why don't you go and tell mommy?"

My wife fished the toothbrush out of the toilet and threw it in the trash can. Cameron looked puzzled. His expression was one of reflection or, perhaps, regret. After thinking a moment, he ran to our bathroom and emerged with my toothbrush.

I reached for it and said, "That's OK, son. You really don't need to show me what happened."

Cameron replied, "But Dad, we'd better throw your toothbrush in the trash, too, because I dropped it in the toilet last week."

We want and need to be good stewards of the truth. We need to do what's right in the sight of the Lord and also in plain view of people. Have you "dropped anything in the toilet bowl" this week that you need to tell someone about?

Honesty *is* the best policy.

engaging

Have you "dropped anything in the toilet bowl" this week that you need to tell someone about?

Write down the "toothbrushes" you've dropped lately, and resolve to deal with them honestly this week.

empowering

"Jesus went on to make these comments: If you're honest in small things, you'll be honest in big things; If you're a crook in small things, you'll be a crook in big things. If you're not honest in small jobs, who will put you in charge of the store?"—Luke 16:10-12 *(The Message)*

equipping

If you're honest with small matters, you'll be honest with large matters. No matter where the toothbrush has been, it's best to tell the truth.

- When have you been tempted to lie but told the truth instead?
- What happened? How did you feel? Why did you decide to tell the truth?
- What can encourage you to tell the truth the next time you're tempted to lie?

experiencing

Meditate and pray this week about honesty in your life and ministry...

Lord, it's sometimes tempting to cover my mistakes with lies. But you love me no matter how completely I mess up, and I can't hide anything from you. Despite my foibles, you love me. Thank you, God, for your unfailing love. Help me to rest in the assurance of your love instead of resorting to lies. Amen.

Following the Leader

encouraging

My family and I recently visited an amusement park while on vacation. We were enjoying ourselves, but the lines grew longer and longer and the weather grew hotter and hotter.

We eventually arrived at a popular ride to find no shade, a closed door, and a thirty-minute wait until we could get in line to wait some more.

The doors finally opened, and we began the exciting process of snaking through the guided aisles to the front of the ride. I'd grown frustrated by the wait, and I simply did not want to snake back and forth through the chain aisles.

I detached the chain and took a shortcut across about six empty aisles. When I looked back, I was amazed to see that everyone had followed me. Perhaps without even meaning to, they simply had followed the leader.

When you make good choices, children follow. When you make poor choices, children follow. Be sure you're walking the right path because when you turn around, you'll certainly find that we all follow the leader.

Take a few minutes to pray for your leaders—for their protection, safety, and wisdom. Then take a few minutes to pray for your own wisdom and discernment as you teach and empower those you lead.

engaging

Pray for your leaders this week by name. Pray for their protection, safety, and wisdom. Pray for your *own* wisdom and discernment too. As you teach children, you're leading them. You're a leader!

empowering

"Dear brothers and sisters, not many of you should become teachers in the church, for we who teach will be judged by God with greater strictness." —James 3:1 *(NLT)*

equipping

Teaching carries tremendous responsibility. But teachers also have the wonderful opportunity to lead children to love Jesus.

- If the children you care for follow you as their leader, where will they arrive?
- How can you encourage your fellow teachers to lead well?
- Who can you ask to hold you accountable as a teacher who leads children?

experiencing

Meditate and pray this week about leadership in your life and ministry...

Lord, what an awesome responsibility you've given me! Help me not to shrink from my work, but to embrace the opportunity to lead. Grant me wisdom, Lord, and a loving heart. Help me to lead those who follow me ever closer to you. Amen.

encouraging

A hurricane was hitting the East Coast just as my wife and I were trying to leave the area. Our flight out of Washington, D.C., was cancelled, but we discovered that we could catch a flight out of Baltimore—an hour's drive away. So at 2:30 in the morning, we loaded up a car and headed for Baltimore. The rain poured and the wind howled the entire way. But we made it to Baltimore, and, tired and cranky, we boarded the plane.

We sat on the runway for thirty minutes while someone somewhere decided whether we should take off. The rain fell so furiously we couldn't see the airport terminal; the clouds hovered so low we couldn't see the end of the runway. It was clear—at least to *me*—that if we were going to leave, we needed to "floor it" and get out of there. Fast.

Finally the engines revved, and we headed down the runway. At takeoff, the plane bounced and bobbed as we struggled up through the clouds. But suddenly we broke through, and a bright, sunny sky enveloped us and provided a smooth ride.

We've all experienced those hurricane-type days, when it seems that everyone we meet is raining on us. We have a choice: Will we climb aboard, buckle up, rev the engines, and take off? With our noses up and wings out, we can soar above the clouds.

And trust me: The view is *much* better up there!

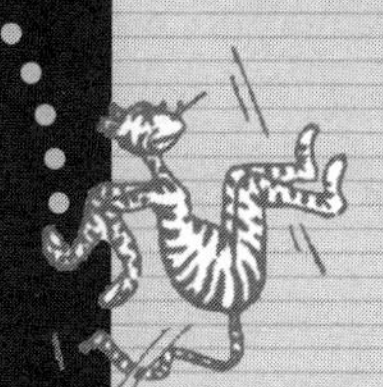

engaging

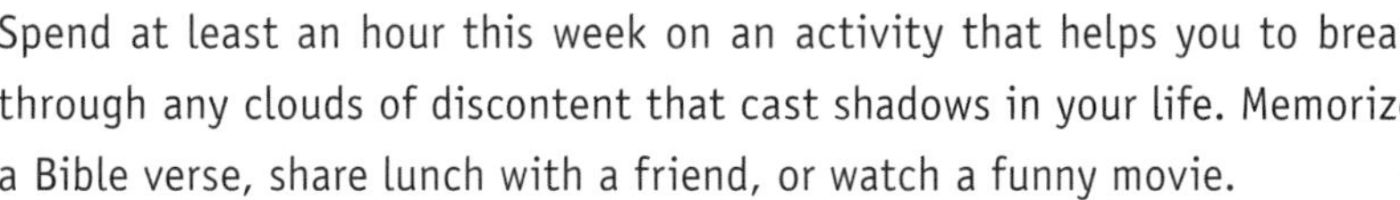

Spend at least an hour this week on an activity that helps you to break through any clouds of discontent that cast shadows in your life. Memorize a Bible verse, share lunch with a friend, or watch a funny movie.

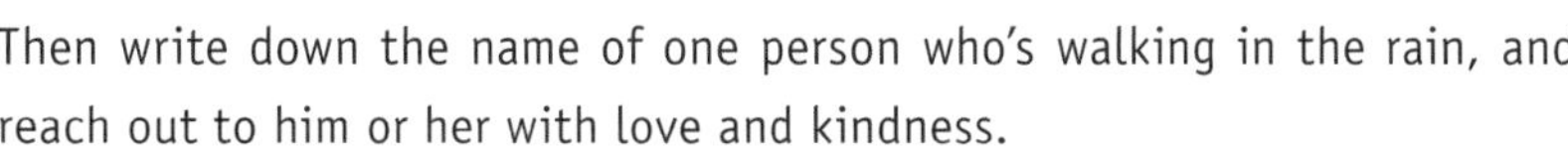

Then write down the name of one person who's walking in the rain, and reach out to him or her with love and kindness.

empowering

"But those who wait upon God get fresh strength. They spread their wings and soar like eagles, they run and don't get tired, they walk and don't lag behind."

—Isaiah 40:31 *(The Message)*

equipping

All of us have those gloomy and cloudy days. The great encouragement for us is that nearly always we can choose to soar above the clouds. It takes courage, a decision, and trust in God.

- Do you feel like you're soaring above the clouds or walking in the rain? Why?

- What could you do in your life right now that would help you to soar above the clouds?

- How can you help others to soar?

experiencing

Meditate and pray this week about the storms in your life and ministry...

Lord, sometimes I feel as though I'm slogging along in a pouring rain. Thunderclouds follow me, and I'm soaked to the bone. Speak to me in those moments, Lord. Encourage me to shake off the rain. Challenge me to evaporate the cloud. Set your rainbow over me, and lift my wings until I soar. Amen.

encouraging

I traveled out of the country recently and re-entered the United States through a customs checkpoint. As I stood in line, I noticed several signs that read, "Please keep foot-and-mouth disease out of the United States."

Though I realize that foot-and-mouth disease is a serious, infectious disease that affects cows and pigs, I couldn't help but chuckle. "We *should* do our part to keep foot-and-mouth disease out of the United States," I said to my wife, "but I hope they don't ask us to keep foot-*in*-mouth disease out. I think I'm a carrier."

Foot-*in*-mouth disease isn't fatal, but it can cause problems. I know this from experience. During times of stress or fatigue, I'm always planting my foot in my mouth, saying exactly the wrong thing to the wrong person for the wrong reason.

Maybe you suffer from foot-in-mouth disease, too, at least occasionally. If so, then I expect you've also learned about the remedy.

It's called an apology for things said...and a sincere desire to control our tongues so we don't experience another outbreak.

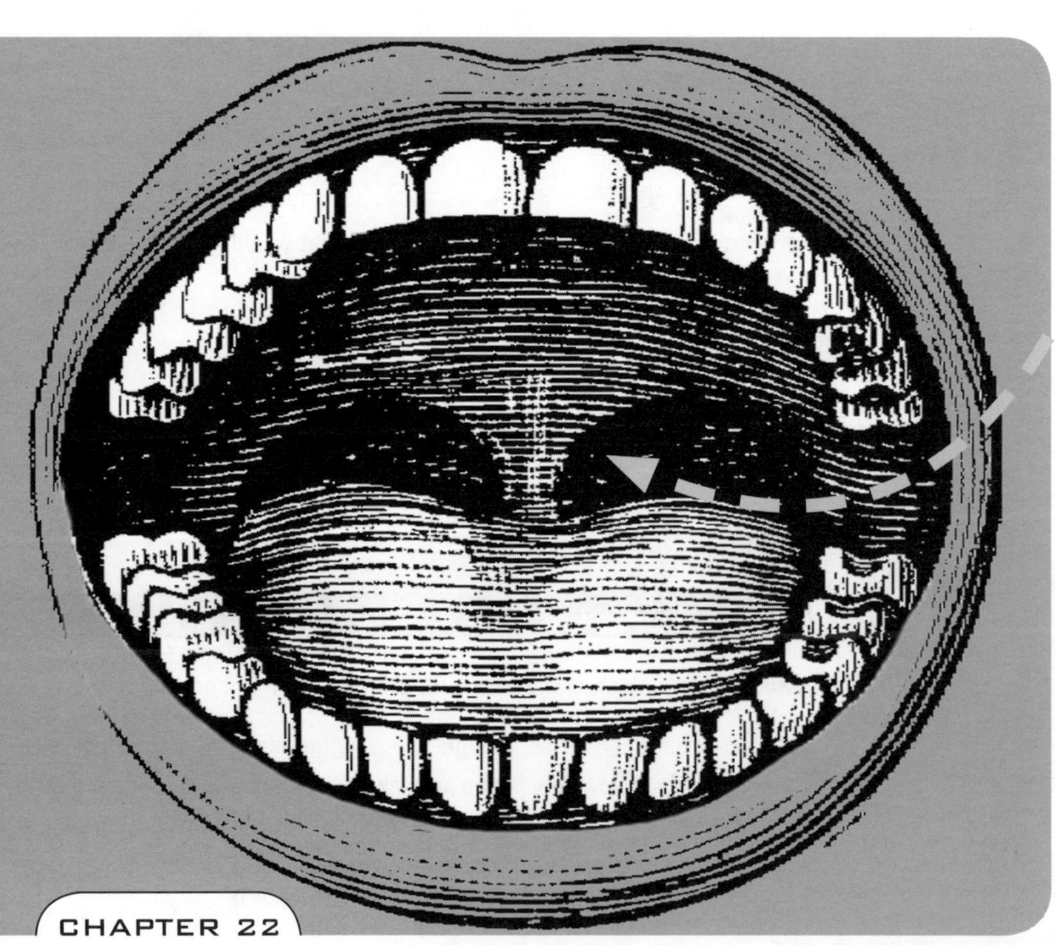

engaging

Do you suffer from foot-in-mouth disease? Read James 3:5-9, and contemplate the importance of the tongue. Consider whether you need to seek forgiveness from someone who has been an unfortunate victim of your foot-in-mouth disease.

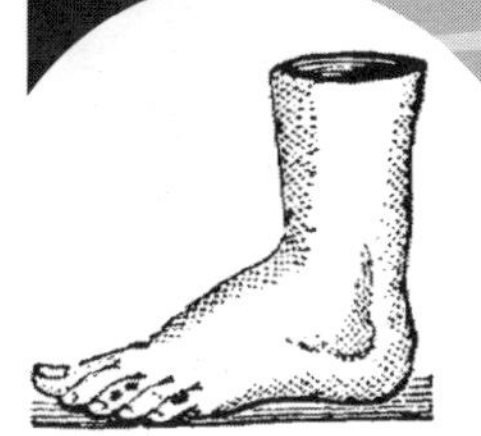

empowering

"Anyone who says he is a Christian but doesn't control his sharp tongue is just fooling himself, and his religion isn't worth much."

—James 1:26 *(TLB)*

equipping

Fortunately, most of us don't seek to harm others with our tongues. With a little preventative medicine—especially Scripture and prayer—we can improve our condition.

- What happened when you last suffered from foot-in-mouth disease?
- When have you successfully prevented yourself from hurting someone with your tongue?
- How does it feel to know that you have that kind of control over your tongue?

experiencing

Meditate and pray this week about controlling your tongue in your life and ministry...

Lord, I find myself asking the same question Paul asked: "Why do I do what I don't want to do?" I don't want to hurt people with my words. I don't mean to gossip or spread rumors. I don't mean to speak without thinking. But sometimes...Help to purify my thoughts, Lord, so that my mouth never has the chance to let slip any words motivated by venom. Thank you for your Spirit that whispers truth to me. Let me do the same for others. Amen.

encouraging

Some friends shared that their youngest child recently began attending kindergarten. This child, like most, has a tendency to speak what's on his mind without considering whether it's appropriate. My friends sent a note with their child for the teacher. It read, "The opinions expressed by this child are not necessarily those of his parents."

The Bible says we are God's children—the Lord's very own kids. I wonder whether God sometimes wants to send a note with us that reads, "The opinions expressed by these children are not necessarily those of their Father."

As God's children, we want to model what our Father teaches. And hallelujah! God has given us the means to do just that.

This week, slow down...think before you speak...and ask yourself, "What would my Father think about these words?" Allow God's Spirit to work through your teaching, your leading, your serving, and your speaking.

The opinions expressed by these children are NOT necessarily those of their Father.

engaging

Let's declare this National Slow Down and Think Week.

This week, before you speak, ask yourself, "What would my Father think about these words?" Allow God's Spirit to work through your teaching, your leading, your serving...*and* the words you speak.

empowering

"You will say the wrong thing if you talk too much—so be sensible and watch what you say."

—Proverbs 10:19 *(CEV)*

equipping

We don't need to be slaves to our own quick speech. We can draw on God's wisdom and strength to control what we say.

- When in the past have you been able to restrain yourself from saying too much? What happened?

- What's your response to knowing that God's Spirit can help you speak carefully?

- How can you model God's words to your kids?

experiencing

Meditate and pray this week about using words carefully in your life and ministry...

Lord, I want people to know you through my words. But sometimes I say too much, and sometimes I don't say enough. Please sharpen my mind and inhabit my thoughts so I'll know when I need to be silent and when I should speak out. Amen.

encouraging

Flying home from a trip, I became unsettled about how...well, *ordinary*...everything felt. Being one of the first passengers on the plane, I was able to watch the flight attendants and the other passengers as they boarded.

Passengers trudged down the aisle, quietly complying with all the rules and regulations concerning their luggage and electronic devices. The flight attendant, with arms crossed, studied her fingernails as she blandly recited from memory the safety features of "our Boeing 737 aircraft."

Everyone was mindlessly going through the motions. I just hoped the pilot was paying more attention.

You know, the message of salvation is way more exciting than the safety features of a Boeing 737. But sometimes we recite God's wondrous promises with all the passion and joy demonstrated by that flight attendant.

Teaching children is a high calling. When we simply go through the motions, we're doing ourselves and our children an injustice. Rekindle the joy of your salvation. Get *enthused* about the honor of sharing the good news with children!

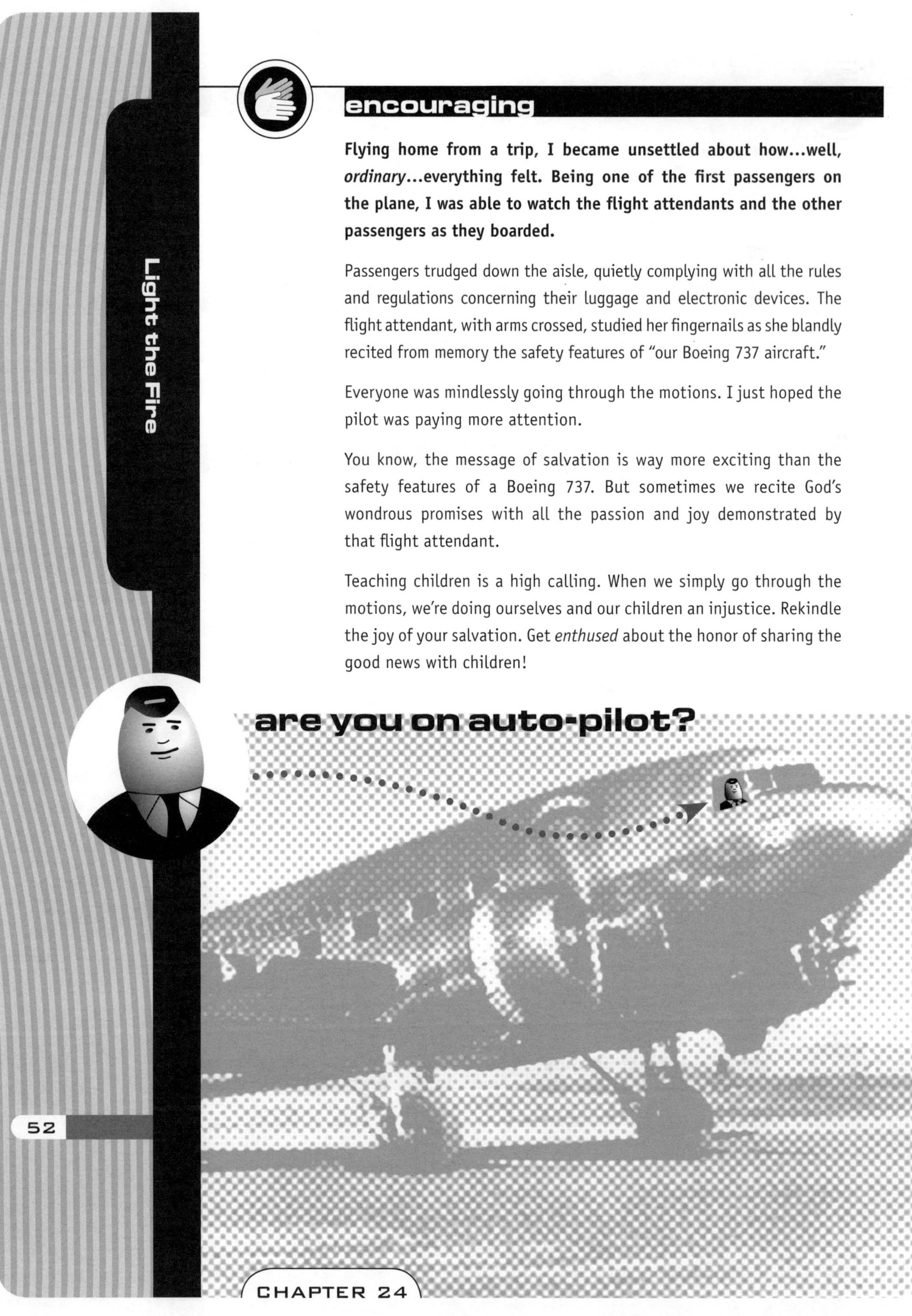

engaging

Get enthused—and help your kids be enthused too! This coming week, plan an out-of-the-ordinary activity to engage kids' attention and fire up their enthusiasm!

empowering

"Give me back the joy of your salvation."

—Psalm 51:12 *(NCV)*

equipping

Remember when you first responded to the life-changing news of what Christ did for you on the cross? Energy and excitement oozed out of you!

What are you oozing these days?

- In which specific areas of your life do you think you're just going through the motions?

- What have you done in the past to rekindle the energy and joy you have in Christ?

- What has God done for you? When you consider those things, how do you feel? How can you let that energize your teaching when you're with children?

experiencing

Meditate and pray this week about passion in your life and ministry...

Lord, I can't believe that I ever feel passionless about what you've done for me. You've done so much! You've given me life and love. You've given me strength and hope. You've given me a future. Thank you, God! Amen.

encouraging

As we fly through life, potential hazards sometimes plant themselves in our way. Just ask Lt. Col. Sam Carter.

Carter was piloting an F-16 fighter jet down a runway at 160 miles per hour when a lost pair of wild pigs wandered into his path. A blur and a bump later, the jet was stranded in a ditch and the pilot was ejected from his seat two hundred feet in the air.

The pigs were killed. The pilot was bruised. The $16 million jet was obliterated.

Maybe you tried to "take off" one morning lately, only to hit an obstacle that required you to eject from your day. You survived, but your plans for the day were a wreck. You hit obstacles that put your plane in a ditch. It happens.

And, like it or not, it happens *frequently*. This week, if you're rolling down the runway and feel an uncomfortable bump, just go ahead and eject. Maybe God has other plans for your day.

Pause and take a deep breath. Stay calm. Pray for a quick moment. Then float back to earth and ask God how he wants to use you in the midst of the traffic jam, at the newly announced all-day meeting, or at the muffler shop while you wait for repairs.

engaging

The next time your day comes unraveled, ask God what he has in mind for you. Seek to serve him wherever you are, whatever is happening. And do this, too: Look for a fellow teacher whose face betrays his or her panic. Give that person a hug, and say a brief prayer asking God to use that teacher.

empowering

"Then God will strengthen you with his own great power. And you will not give up when troubles come, but you will be patient."

—Colossians 1:11 *(ICB)*

equipping

Sometimes when we try to avoid hitting obstacles in our paths, we do more harm than good. Unmet expectations, unresolved conflict, unfulfilled dreams—God can help us boldly face obstacles we can't avoid—and avoid those that seem to frequently wander into our paths.

- What are the "wild pigs" on the runway of your life?

- How are they affecting you?

- What can you do to deal with them *before* you collide with them?

experiencing

Meditate and pray this week about obstacles in your life and ministry...

Lord, you are more concerned with my character than my comfort. I recognize that I need to confront some uncomfortable obstacles. Help me to hold on to you—to your Word and your will—during this wild ride. Amen.

encouraging

Why would a man leave nearly a quarter million dollars behind and instead carry away three oranges? We'll never know for certain, but here's my thoughts on the matter.

Major Arthur Godfrey Peuchen had the good fortune—or so he thought—of securing first-class passage on the historic maiden launch of the Titanic. Peuchen had traversed the Atlantic dozens of times, but a maiden launch wasn't to be missed.

One evening after dinner, a steward told Peuchen the Titanic had struck an iceberg. Before heading to a lifeboat, Peuchen returned to his cabin. Was it to get the $200,000 in stocks and bonds he'd rought? To gather up the jewelry? Or to grab the gifts he'd purchased for his children?

No. Peuchen returned to his cabin for three little oranges.

Circumstances aboard the Titanic had transformed his values. For this wealthy man from a privileged background, the life-sustaining value of oranges took precedence over money and jewels.

What values guide the ministry in which you're involved? What values prompt you to *be* involved? Brainstorm with fellow teachers about the values that direct your work. Then spend a few minutes alone, considering those values that guide your involvement in ministry.

engaging

God values children! Is that what prompts your involvement in children's ministry, or is there something else? Take a few minutes to think about what guides your values in children's ministry. Be sure your values align with God's values.

empowering

"Whoever has a mature faith should think this way. And if you think differently, God will show you how to think. However, we should be guided by what we have learned so far."

—Philippians 3:15-16 *(God's Word)*

equipping

When values are clear, decisions become far easier.

- How have your values helped you to make decisions in the past?
- What difficult decisions is life asking you to make?
- What values can help you make those decisions?

experiencing

Meditate and pray this week about values in your life and ministry...

Lord, thank you for those experiences and decisions that serve to clarify my values. Continue to frame and shape my values so they mirror yours. Teach me, and help me to learn with open eyes and ears. Amen.

encouraging

Your team played an amazing basketball season. You coached them to twenty-one wins and only five losses, which earned a slot in the Georgia high school basketball tournament. They dribbled, hooked, and slammed their way to the finals, where in a come-from-behind push they won the state title.

What a season!

A few days later, you watch the tape of that final game. You want to savor the sweet victory all over again. As you watch, something catches your eye. You rewind the tape. You watch, then rewind the tape again.

Your heart sinks into your shoes. You've discovered that an ineligible player from your team was on the court for forty-five seconds of a critical post-season game.

What would you do?

If you were Coach Cleveland Stroud, you'd phone the Georgia High School Association and report the violation. It cost his team the victory and the trophy.

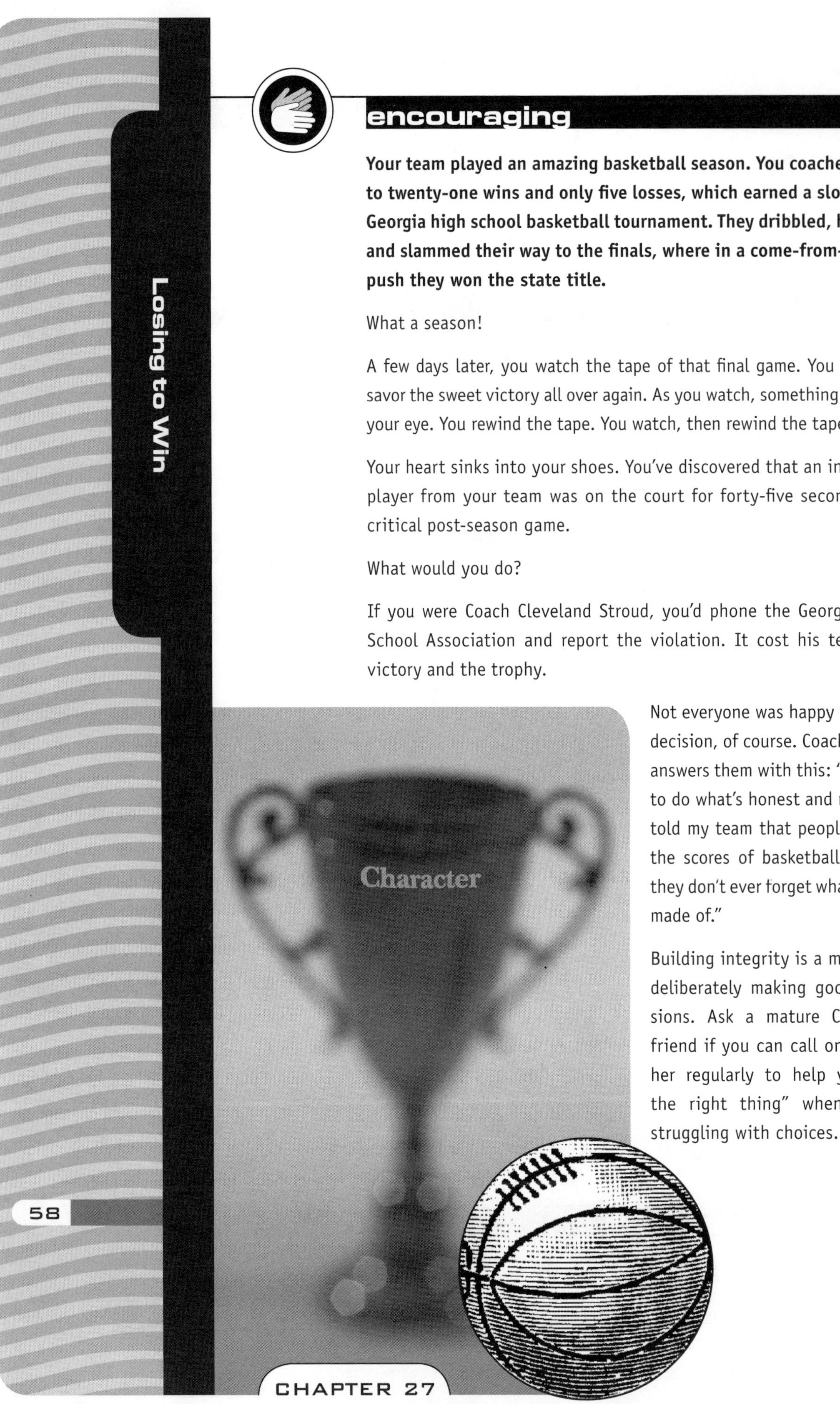

Not everyone was happy with his decision, of course. Coach Stroud answers them with this: "You got to do what's honest and right...I told my team that people forget the scores of basketball games; they don't ever forget what you're made of."

Building integrity is a matter of deliberately making good decisions. Ask a mature Christian friend if you can call on him or her regularly to help you "do the right thing" when you're struggling with choices.

engaging

The kids you teach may forget most of what you tell them, but they'll long remember your example. Ask a mature Christian friend if you can call on him or her regularly to help you "do the right thing" when you're struggling with choices.

empowering

"A righteous man who walks in his integrity—
How blessed are his sons after him."

—Proverbs 20:7 *(New American Standard Bible)*

equipping

"Character is what you are in the dark" (attributed to Dwight L. Moody). Our Creator sees our struggles and delights in answering our prayers for wisdom.

- When have you made a "Coach Stroud" decision? What was that like?

- What examples of your own integrity encourage you as you face new decisions?

- Which of God's promises encourage you as you face difficult decisions?

experiencing

Meditate and pray this week about integrity in your life and ministry...

Lord, thank you for examples of ethical decision making in this world. I could get caught in the trap of thinking "everybody's doing it," but then I'm reminded of what a lie that is. You're always watching, always reaching out to me with a helping hand. Thank you, God. Thank you for helping me to build integrity by making decisions in your light. Amen.

encouraging

The youth from our church used to visit a senior care home once a week. The kids would talk and listen, and flip through picture albums. It was a rich time of fellowship for all.

One time, our students created a special holiday program for the residents. During the show, one of our adult leaders was trying to coax a resident to participate. Despite encouraging words, the gentleman wouldn't budge. Our leader, seeking to reassure the man, asked, "Do you know who I am?"

"No," the gentleman replied. "But if you go to the front desk, they'll tell you."

Great answer! We all need folks who'll help us know who we are—and that we belong.

Every day this week, repeat these words aloud: "I wake up each day knowing that there are people I can lean on, people who know my name, people who can offer me help, people who can guide me, people who can pray for me, people who can laugh with me, people who can rejoice with me. I wake up each day knowing that people care about me and my life."

That's true if you're in the kingdom of God, and especially true if you serve in children's ministry. You're *surrounded* by caring people who can encourage you—and who you can encourage.

Who have you encouraged today?

engaging

Every day this week, repeat these words aloud: "I wake up each day knowing that there are people I can lean on, people who know my name, people who can offer me help, people who can guide me, people who can pray for me, people who can laugh with me, people who can rejoice with me. I wake up each day knowing that people care about me and my life."

What can you do to enter more fully into that caring community?

I know there are people I can lean on.

empowering

"They worshiped together regularly at the Temple each day, met in small groups in homes for Communion, and shared their meals with great joy and thankfulness."

—Acts 2:46 *(TLB)*

equipping

We all need a safe place to share life's hurts, struggles, pains, victories, and joys. We all need friends to share common life experiences with, to offer and receive support.

- Who are the people who encourage you?

- How can your ministry team create an environment that's safe and encouraging?

- Who do you need to reach out to with the words "you belong"? (It may even be yourself!)

experiencing

Meditate and pray this week about community in your life and ministry...

Lord, I rejoice at all the fellowship opportunities your family provides me. Still, sometimes I feel alone...separated from your community. I feel as though I don't belong anywhere—or with anyone. But I always belong with you. Remind me, God, to open my heart to you and to others who are seeking community just as much as I am. Amen.

encouraging

Every summer, our church sends some four hundred kids to camp—all at the same time. We've even developed a special sign-in process to get all those kids onto the right buses.

During one pre-camp meeting, Cynthia proposed a new way of signing in the campers. To be honest, I couldn't have disagreed more. *The old strategy works just fine,* I thought. *Why change it now?* So I told my colleague that I didn't agree but that she could do what she wanted.

The busy day arrived, and throngs of kids and parents crowded the parking lot. I stood to the side watching the new sign-in system unfold before my eyes.

Like a hot knife moving through butter, the campers signed in and got on their buses. Her idea worked! In fact, at least ten parents mentioned how much they appreciated the new sign-in system. I believe their exact words were "It was much better than last year."

Read Proverbs 12:15. Reflect on the times you've acted without being open to counsel from others. Then commit that verse to memory to help you recall what a gift another person's counsel can be.

engaging

Read Proverbs 12:15. Reflect on the times you've acted without counsel from others. Then commit the verse to memory to help you remember the wonderful gift of another person's counsel.

empowering

"A stubborn fool considers his own way the right one, but a person who listens to advice is wise."—Proverbs 12:15 *(God's Word)*

equipping

All of us together are smarter than one of us alone. Our success in teaching or leading children depends, in part, on listening to the wise counsel of our co-workers.

- What co-workers and friends have acted as wise, wonderful counselors in your life? (Be sure to thank them!)
- How can you develop an attitude of humility so you can receive wise counsel from others?
- You're a counselor to others too! In which areas do you need to further develop your voice and skills as a counselor?

experiencing

Meditate and pray this week about listening to advice in your life and ministry...

Lord, you've promised to grant wisdom to those who ask. I seek your wisdom in these areas...Help me to listen for your answer, even if it comes through the advice of a friend or co-worker. Thank you for your wise, wonderful counsel. Amen.

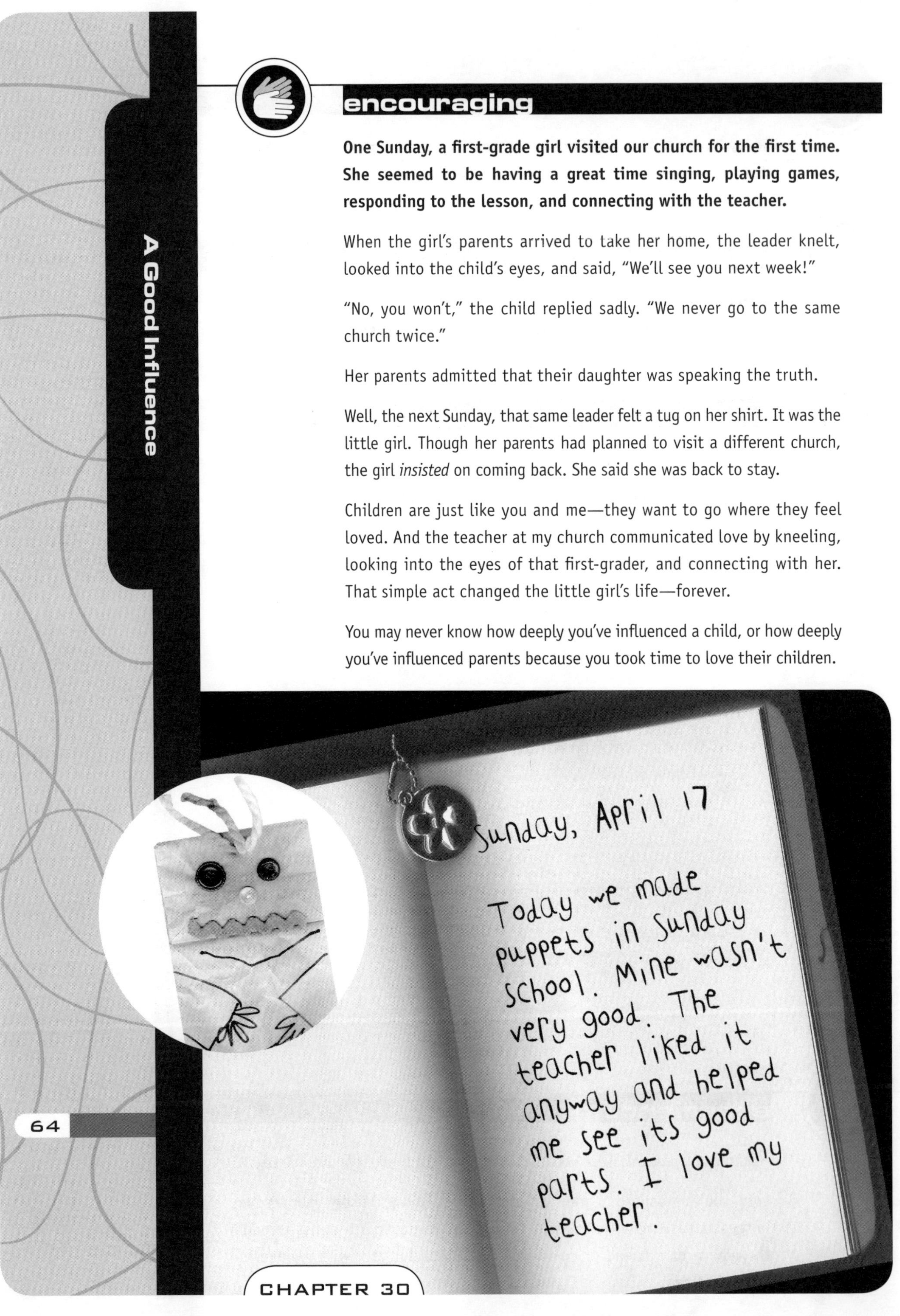

A Good Influence

encouraging

One Sunday, a first-grade girl visited our church for the first time. She seemed to be having a great time singing, playing games, responding to the lesson, and connecting with the teacher.

When the girl's parents arrived to take her home, the leader knelt, looked into the child's eyes, and said, "We'll see you next week!"

"No, you won't," the child replied sadly. "We never go to the same church twice."

Her parents admitted that their daughter was speaking the truth.

Well, the next Sunday, that same leader felt a tug on her shirt. It was the little girl. Though her parents had planned to visit a different church, the girl *insisted* on coming back. She said she was back to stay.

Children are just like you and me—they want to go where they feel loved. And the teacher at my church communicated love by kneeling, looking into the eyes of that first-grader, and connecting with her. That simple act changed the little girl's life—forever.

You may never know how deeply you've influenced a child, or how deeply you've influenced parents because you took time to love their children.

engaging

Today, list three ways you'd like to influence children. Keep your list handy as a reminder of the influence you have as a teacher.

empowering

"I'm giving you a new commandment: Love each other in the same way that I have loved you."—John 13:34 *(God's Word)*

equipping

Loving children as Jesus loves you—what a fun privilege!

- Which teachers or leaders have influenced you? How do you feel about those people?
- What's your reaction to the thought that you may influence a child in the same way?
- How can you do a better job of loving children as Jesus loves you?

experiencing

Meditate and pray this week about the influence you wield in your life and ministry...

Lord, serving you carries massive responsibilities. I recognize that I influence the kids I teach—and their parents. Help me always to be mindful of my influence. Thank you for the privilege of serving these little ones—and you. Amen.

encouraging

When I was in elementary school, my mom dragged me to church. Neither of us were Christians, but she always said, "We live selfishly all week, so we can at least set aside an hour to give back to God."

The church was small, the classroom ordinary, and the piano out of tune. I don't remember specific lessons, but I remember having fun.

I *especially* remember the people—lots of high fives and smiling faces that were glad to see me. They remembered my name. They truly loved kids. My mom didn't have to drag me for long because I *wanted* to be there. For the people.

During our two-year involvement in that church, I didn't become a Christian. But those smiles and kind hearts planted seeds that eventually blossomed in me until I surrendered my life to Christ.

I wish I knew who those people were.

I'd love for them to know that they've changed my life.

engaging

There are very few notes we tuck away and keep for a lifetime. This week, write three of those for three people who showed you God's love when you were a child. Maybe those people have passed on or lost touch with you, and you can't send the notes. Write the notes anyway. It will help you bring into focus how God uses adults to share his love with children.

Those people changed my life.

empowering

"Greet one another with a kiss of love. Peace be to you all who are in Christ."—1 Peter 5:14 *(NASB)*

equipping

One person—you!—can make a difference in a child's life. Working together to share God's love with children can make an even greater impact.

- How does your ministry team work together to shower children with love?
- How do you feel when you think about all the lives you're touching through your service?
- What specific actions can you adopt to share God's love with kids that come through your church?

experiencing

Meditate and pray this week about sharing love with kids through your life and ministry...

Lord, what an honor and responsibility you've given me to work with children! I pray that your love for them will shine through me. Specifically, I pray for these children...Help me to shepherd the children well so that they can know you better. Amen.

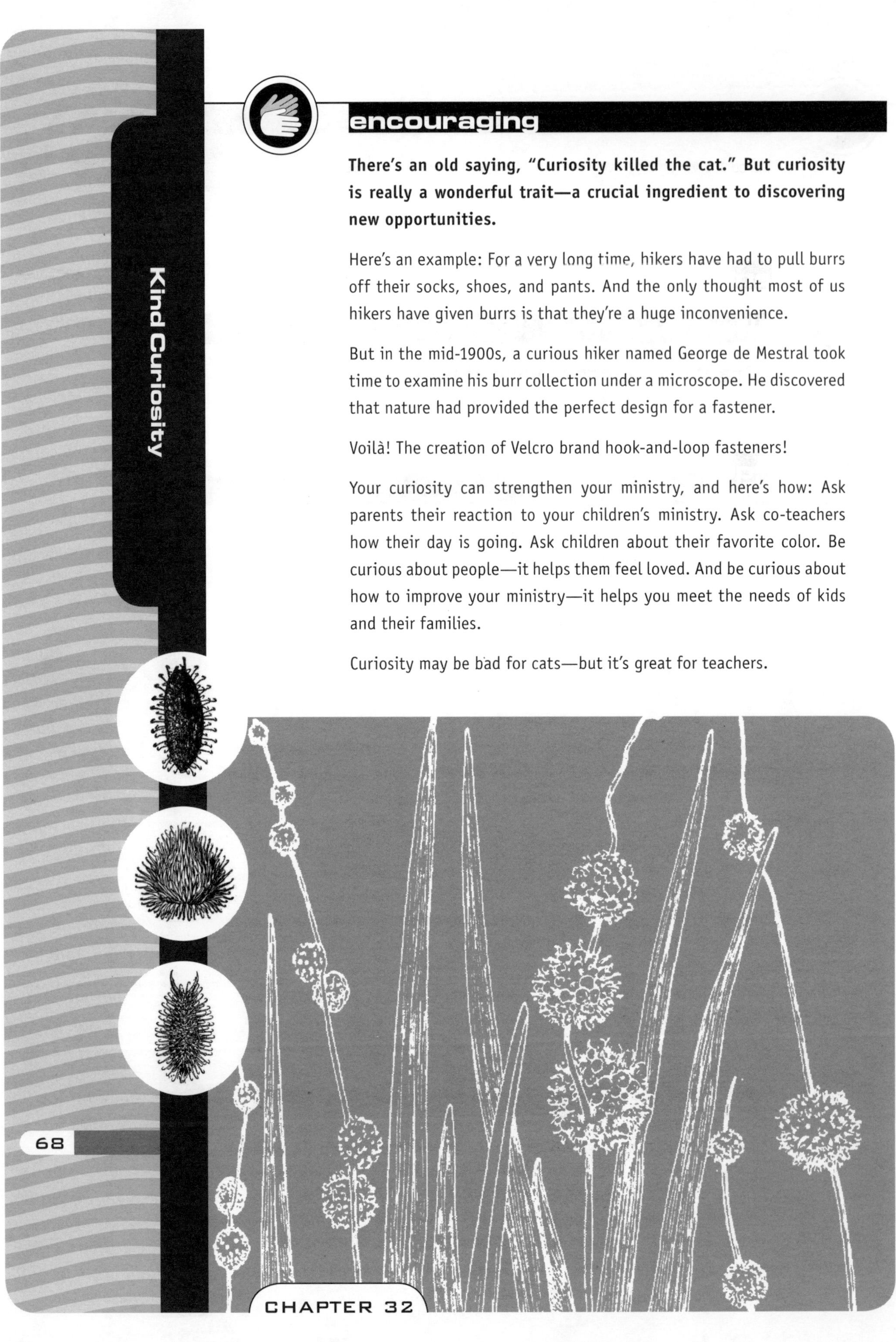

encouraging

There's an old saying, "Curiosity killed the cat." But curiosity is really a wonderful trait—a crucial ingredient to discovering new opportunities.

Here's an example: For a very long time, hikers have had to pull burrs off their socks, shoes, and pants. And the only thought most of us hikers have given burrs is that they're a huge inconvenience.

But in the mid-1900s, a curious hiker named George de Mestral took time to examine his burr collection under a microscope. He discovered that nature had provided the perfect design for a fastener.

Voilà! The creation of Velcro brand hook-and-loop fasteners!

Your curiosity can strengthen your ministry, and here's how: Ask parents their reaction to your children's ministry. Ask co-teachers how their day is going. Ask children about their favorite color. Be curious about people—it helps them feel loved. And be curious about how to improve your ministry—it helps you meet the needs of kids and their families.

Curiosity may be bad for cats—but it's great for teachers.

engaging

Be curious this week. Ask a child's parent, "What was the most meaningful part of today's service?" Ask a child, "What's your favorite part of our program?" Ask your co-teachers, "What worked well for you today?"

empowering

"If any of you needs wisdom to know what you should do, you should ask God, and he will give it to you."

—James 1:5a *(God's Word)*

equipping

Curiosity opens new doors. Future ministry possibilities and improvements to current systems flow out of asking questions and seeking information.

- When in the past has your curiosity led you to a great idea? How did that happen?
- What "burrs" are sticking to you right now?
- What can you learn from those burrs—and dealing with them in new ways?

experiencing

Meditate and pray this week about curiosity in your life and ministry...

Lord, thank you for that little itch at the back of my brain that says, "We can do this better." It's fun to be a part of positive change! Please bless me—and my co-teachers—with your wisdom so we can continue improving for your sake. Amen.

encouraging

A popular story illustrates the perils of careless speech.

It seems General Motors decided to expand its market for the Chevy Nova. Auto executives decided to introduce the Nova to Spanish-speaking countries.

They spent a fortune on advertising, but sales remained completely flat. The cars just weren't selling.

Finally, someone discovered the reason for the fiasco. The words "No va" translate as "no go" in Spanish. Who wants to buy a car that doesn't go?

We constantly communicate with our kids and their parents—verbally and nonverbally. How much of what we say gets lost in translation?

Pay keen attention to the language you use when talking to your kids. Are you using words that make sense to them? Do your actions support what you're teaching about God's love? Every once in a while, ask a child, "What do you think about what I just said?" or "What words would *you* use to share this Bible verse with a friend?"

You'll encourage the child by asking—and do yourself a favor too.

engaging

Do the things you say to kids make sense to the children? Are your words "kid-friendly"? You won't know unless you ask. Translating God's truth to a child's level of understanding can be daunting—but always rewarding and worth the effort!

Ask a child this week to tell you what he or she learned from your lesson. Be warned: You may not hear what you want to hear. But use the experience as an opportunity to grow in your ability as a teacher!

empowering

"Just say 'yes' and 'no.' When you manipulate words to get your own way, you go wrong."

—Matthew 5:37 (*The Message*)

equipping

No matter how creative our programming, how loving and sensitive our demeanor, or how far-reaching our advertising, speaking a different language from your kids and parents means the program is a "no-go."

- When have you been on the receiving end of someone's confusing communication? What happened?

- When have you successfully translated what began as miscommunication?

- How can you evaluate whether your words are coming across as you intend?

experiencing

Meditate and pray this week about clear communication in your life and ministry...

Lord, in our ministry, so many different worlds collide. I'm an adult trying to communicate with children. Some kids and parents are from places or even cultures unfamiliar to me. The meaning of different "church words" or theological terms changes depending upon who I'm talking to. In the midst of all this confusion, direct my speech. Help me to clearly communicate so that children can learn about you. Amen.

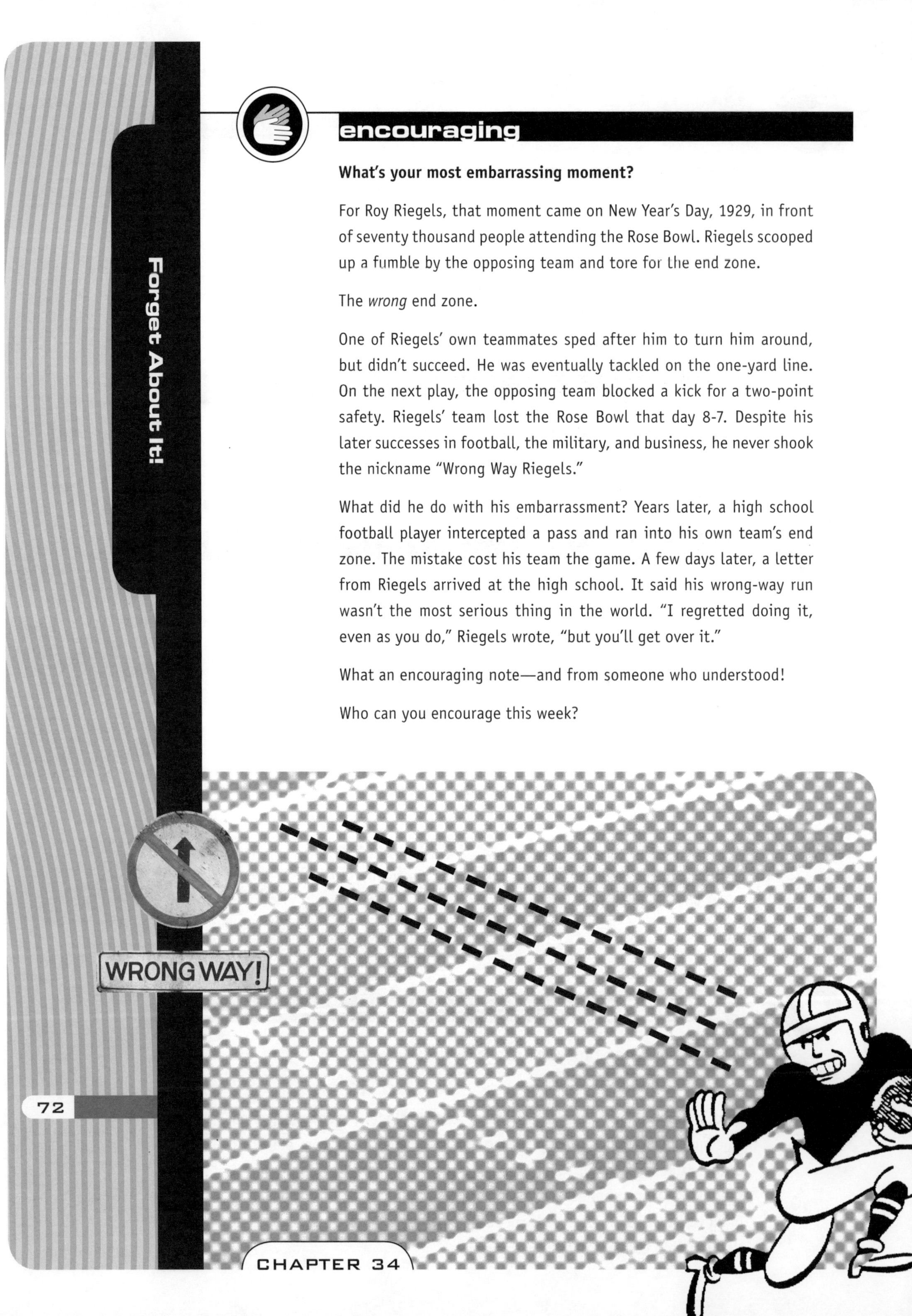

encouraging

What's your most embarrassing moment?

For Roy Riegels, that moment came on New Year's Day, 1929, in front of seventy thousand people attending the Rose Bowl. Riegels scooped up a fumble by the opposing team and tore for the end zone.

The *wrong* end zone.

One of Riegels' own teammates sped after him to turn him around, but didn't succeed. He was eventually tackled on the one-yard line. On the next play, the opposing team blocked a kick for a two-point safety. Riegels' team lost the Rose Bowl that day 8-7. Despite his later successes in football, the military, and business, he never shook the nickname "Wrong Way Riegels."

What did he do with his embarrassment? Years later, a high school football player intercepted a pass and ran into his own team's end zone. The mistake cost his team the game. A few days later, a letter from Riegels arrived at the high school. It said his wrong-way run wasn't the most serious thing in the world. "I regretted doing it, even as you do," Riegels wrote, "but you'll get over it."

What an encouraging note—and from someone who understood!

Who can you encourage this week?

engaging

Who can you encourage this week? Select one child or parent—maybe someone who looks a little down—and offer a kind word. Seize opportunities to lift spirits and breathe life into a discouraged soul.

And if no one looks discouraged, offer encouragement anyway. We don't always let our discouragements show. Everyone you meet today will be carrying a burden of some sort.

empowering

"Worry is a heavy load, but a kind word cheers you up."

—Proverbs 12:25 *(NCV)*

equipping

A smile, bright eyes, a joyful look—a kind countenance melts away discouragement. A kind word has healing power.

- How have someone else's kind words changed your outlook?
- How have you been able to offer encouragement to those around you?
- Who in particular would you like to encourage today?

experiencing

Meditate and pray this week about encouraging others in your life and ministry...

Lord, a mistake or conflict can drain joy right out of me. As I look around, I see people drained of joy. You are the God of all comfort. I want to learn from you how to comfort others. Give me the courage to smile, say a kind word, and encourage others. Amen.

encouraging

Did you know that your outlook on life could affect your health?

Researchers studying a possible link between hopelessness and carotid atherosclerosis—the narrowing of the arteries—found a dramatic increase in heart disease in men who remained hopeless over the course of the four-year study.

The basic difference between optimism and despair is mindset: Is the glass half full or half empty? For your physical *and* spiritual health, train yourself to see glasses that are half full! The Bible holds wonderful promises, and faith brings hope.

Give your despair to God. On an index card, write down whatever is clouding your life with discouragement and hopelessness. Place the card on a bathroom mirror, by your bed, or in your car. Every time you see the card, give those troubles to the Lord.

Is your outlook healthy?

engaging

Feel hopeless? Give that despair to God. You need to, for at least two reasons: First, because you need peace and God wants to give peace to you. Second, you can't lead children into a faithful relationship with God unless you're relying on God yourself.

Place your index card where you'll see it this week. And deliberately, proactively take your concerns to God.

empowering

"Give all your worries and cares to God, for he cares about what happens to you."

—1 Peter 5:7 *(NLT)*

equipping

Being optimistic is related to faith—not how much faith you have, but in *whom* you place your faith.

- How has God fulfilled promises in the past?

- How does it make you feel to know that you can cast your burdens upon the Lord?

- What are some ways you can give your troubles to God?

experiencing

Meditate and pray this week about optimism in your life and ministry...

Lord, thank you for being faithful to keep your promises and guard our hearts. Thank you for loving us so much that you not only understand our worries, but encourage us to cast our cares upon you. You are my hope! Amen.

encouraging

At one time, physiologists generally agreed: Human beings could not safely run a mile in less than four minutes.

But Roger Bannister disagreed.

On May 6, 1954, years of conventional wisdom and a psychological barrier shattered as Bannister ran a mile in 3 minutes, 59.4 seconds. Less than two months later, *another* runner broke the four-minute mile...then another...then another. Within about three years, sixteen runners had broken the barrier.

A pacesetter is a trendsetter, a barrier breaker—someone who crashes through quitting points. The most amazing thing about Bannister's story is not that he broke the four-minute mile, but that so many *others* did after he paved the way.

As you teach children, you're paving the way. Just as experts didn't expect Bannister to be able to beat a four-minute mile, people don't expect you to react to some children with love. When you handle a tough situation, care for an uncaring child, love although you're not being loved, you're breaking barriers. When you model these behaviors for children, you're *shattering* barriers.

Identify one situation in which you can surprise a child with love this week. Identify another situation in which you can set a Christlike example.

engaging

Who can you surprise with loving behavior? Identify another situation in which you can set a Christlike example for others. Commit to following through on your ideas. Call a friend, and ask him or her to support you and hold you accountable.

empowering

"Remember your leaders who have spoken God's word to you. Think about how their lives turned out, and imitate their faith."

—Hebrews 13:7 *(God's Word)*

equipping

As a teacher, you're in a high-visibility position. Parents watch you to see how you relate to their kids and to see how their kids are imitating you. Kids watch you so they can model your behavior.

- What's your reaction to this?

- Who are you watching? What are you learning from those people?

- What specific behaviors do you want to adopt in order to pave the way for those who are watching you?

experiencing

Meditate and pray this week about being a pacesetter for others in your life and ministry...

Lord, I'm a bit intimidated by the idea of being a pacesetter. Are you sure I can do this? It's reassuring to know I'm not alone. You are my pacesetter, my guide, and my shepherd. I will follow you. Then others can follow me. Amen.

encouraging

When my kids were four years old, they performed during an end-of-the-year program at preschool. I remember chuckling, thinking, *This has got to be the worst program ever!* Kids fell down on stage, wandered around, sang off-key, and simply stood still—doing nothing.

At the program's conclusion, all the parents—including me—jumped to their feet and wildly clapped and cheered. Why?

Our standing ovation was not based on our kids' performance. It was based on our relationship with them. They're our kids! We love them for who they are—not for how they perform.

The same can be said about God's love for us. Sometimes you may sing off-key, you may fall down or wander off the stage. But God gives you a standing ovation anyway!

Let's hear it for teachers!

engaging

Gather with your fellow teachers. Take turns applauding wildly for one another this week!

empowering

"And before the world was made, God decided to make us his own children through Jesus Christ. That was what he wanted and what pleased him."

—Ephesians 1:5 *(ICB)*

equipping

Remember today to bask in the love that the Lord of the universe has for you—just the way you are.

- How does it make you feel to know that the Lord of the universe is applauding you?
- For what do you need to forgive yourself? to ask others to forgive you?
- For what do you need to give yourself an ovation?

experiencing

Meditate and pray this week about recognizing God's love in your life and ministry...

Lord, thank you.

Thank you for loving me when I succeed and when I fail.

Thank you for loving me when I do the right thing and when I do the wrong thing.

Thank you for loving me consistently and unconditionally.

Thank you, God, for loving me.

Amen.

encouraging

Do you remember the TV show *Gilligan's Island?* I grew up with the castaways and fondly remember their crazy antics. Recent advertising campaigns have used the show's theme song, and I've been reminded how much I enjoyed the show.

What was its appeal? People could identify with the endearing characters, certainly. But even more important, I think, was the story itself. Shipwrecked on an island, the characters didn't always get along. But they always needed each other. They had to work together to survive and to build the best life possible. They were loyal.

You share an "island" with your fellow ministry workers. You lead together, teach together, and serve together though you're from different states or countries and have different personalities and gifts. Christ is your common bond.

First Thessalonians 5:11 reminds us, "So comfort each other and give each other strength, just as you are doing now" (ICB).

What does it mean to "give each other strength"? Around our church, it starts with encouraging others with an uplifting high five, hug, or handshake.

What's it mean in *your* church?

engaging

This week, give strength to at least ten people who share the island of *your* life. How? It may be a call, a note, or a dozen donuts brought in for your co-workers along with an encouraging word.

Who's on your list? How will you strengthen the people on your list?

empowering

"Finally, all of you should live together in peace. Try to understand each other. Love each other as brothers. Be kind and humble."

—1 Peter 3:8 *(ICB)*

equipping

Working with your co-teachers, you exemplify the body of Christ. As you serve children, parents, and each other, you accomplish God's work.

- What happens to your relationship when you give strength to a co-teacher?

- How do you feel when a co-teacher praises you or listens to you?

- How can you and your co-teachers develop a greater sense of loyalty for one another?

experiencing

Meditate and pray this week about loyalty in your life and ministry...

Lord, thank you for the wonderful people with whom I serve. Help me to be mindful of them so I can add my strength to theirs when they need it. Help me learn to ask for their help when I'm short of strength. Help us to focus on the common bond we share in Christ, rather than focusing on our differences. Amen.

encouraging

One Sunday morning just before our 9:45 service, I noticed that several lines had formed in front of classrooms. It appeared that check-in was progressing slowly.

I headed to the nearest line to encourage the waiting parents and kids. I suggested that they consider coming to the 8:00 service, when attendance is a bit less. Each child's parents responded that the child *insisted* on spending the morning with Mr. Chuck.

To the next line I went with the same suggestion. Again, it was met with resistance. "I would attend another service, but my child won't let me," parents repeated. "My child wants to see Miss Shelly."

Not one child that day said, "Miss Becky has a great knowledge of Scripture. I'd like to be in her group so I can ponder the wonders of exegesis." I doubt they ever will. Kids don't line up to hear great lessons—sorry. They come back again and again because they connect with a particular teacher. They come back because of who you *are,* not because of what you *do.*

Who *are* you in the Lord—and how will you share that with children?

they come back again and again
because they connect
with a particular teacher

engaging

Select three qualities you hope kids will mention when they're describing you. Now for each quality, identify one way you can demonstrate it in your teaching.

empowering

"Follow my example, as I follow the example of Christ." —1 Corinthians 11:1 *(NCV)*

equipping

Leading children requires we lead with a sense of calling and passion, and connect through caring.

- What skills or gifts do you have that make you a special teacher to kids?

- How can you develop those skills and gifts so you can connect even better with kids?

- Who at your church can help you develop those skills and gifts? What might that person say if you called him or her this week?

experiencing

Meditate and pray this week about the gifts you bring to your life and ministry...

Lord, I'm blessed to be able to work with children. Thank you for giving me gifts and skills that help me connect with kids. Further develop those gifts in me, please, so that through me, children can connect with you. Amen.

encouraging

When we make comparisons, they can come back to haunt us. Consider a joke that was circulating not too long ago:

Microsoft gazillionaire Bill Gates compared the auto industry to the computer industry, saying, "If GM had kept up with technology like the computer industry has, we would all be driving $25 cars that get 1,000 miles to the gallon."

GM's response, according to the joke, was swift. The company's president countered that if the auto industry had developed as the computer industry had, we would all be driving cars that crash at least twice a day and die for no reason.

Comparisons may make us look better—in the short run. The Bible says to forget about comparisons, though. God created each of us to be unique. We have special abilities, personalities, and gifts so we can serve God together. Rest assured, God didn't leave anything out.

And he didn't leave any*one* out, either—including you!

engaging

Make a mental list of your fellow teachers. For several of them—and for yourself—think of three or four abilities that they bring to your church's ministry. Then thank God for your colleagues. And thank your colleagues directly, too!

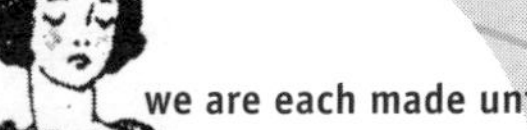

empowering

"I will give thanks to you because I have been so amazingly and miraculously made. Your works are miraculous, and my soul is fully aware of this." —Psalm 139:14 *(God's Word)*

equipping

For every skill or ability you possess, you'll find someone who's better at it and someone who's worse. Comparing yourself to others can rot your self-confidence...or your humility. It's a problem either way.

What, in your mind, do you need to hand over to God when it comes to comparing yourself with someone else?

- When are you most tempted to compare yourself to others?
- How can you transform those thoughts into something more positive?
- With what words can you thank God for your unique talents?

experiencing

Meditate and pray this week about comparisons in your life and ministry...

Lord, you made me and know me. You knit me together. You created me as unique and endowed me with talents. No one is quite like me. When I'm tempted to compare myself to others, remind me of the futility of making comparisons. Help me instead to focus on working well alongside your other children to serve you. Amen.

encouraging

On the evening of August 3, 1992, eight men lined up for the first semifinal of the 400-meter race at the Olympic Games in Barcelona.

Derek Redmond, a British runner and a medal contender, burst out of the blocks as if he'd been shot out of a rifle. All the years of training and all the races he'd run to prepare him for this moment were carrying him toward his goal—the finish line.

Then Redmond's hamstring muscle ripped, and, 250 meters from the finish, he collapsed onto the track.

Long moments passed as he grimaced in pain. Then, slowly, Redmond got up and limped for the finish line.

The other runners were done, the race finished—but not for Redmond. And not for someone who loved him. With 100 meters left, Redmond's father ran from the stands and put his arm around his son's shoulders. And in what has become a symbol of the Olympic ideals of perseverance and determination, the two men slowly finished the race—together.

Derek Redmond didn't win a medal that day, but he finished the race a winner. When everyone in the stadium thought he'd give up, Redmond persevered with a fierce determination.

Determination. What is it exactly? To me, it's a relentless will to continue. It's a choice you make to overlook obstacles or simply walk around or jump over them.

The athlete says, "I will play through my pain."

The counselor says, "I will help you though it."

The Sunday school teacher says, "I will make it to the finish line with my kids because I want to be remembered—not for winning a race, but for simply finishing it well."

And sometimes we do have to play through pain. Sometimes getting up and serving kids is every bit as tough as Derek Redmond climbing up off the track that August day. But we do it, every week, every month, every year—because we're determined.

A question for you: What keeps your determination strong?

engaging

What keeps your determination strong when there are challenges as a teacher? When kids don't seem to care or pay attention? When parents seem distant? Share your answer with another children's worker this week—and decide together to encourage each other.

empowering

FINISH

"I am still not all I should be, but I am bringing all my energies to bear on this one thing: Forgetting the past and looking forward to what lies ahead, I strain to reach the end of the race and receive the prize for which God is calling us up to heaven because of what Christ Jesus did for us."—Philippians 3:13-14 *(TLB)*

equipping

As Christians, we don't need to win the race, we just need to finish it. But Paul reminds us to *strain,* to race with determination because of what Christ did for us.

- What obstacles hinder you from finishing the race?
- How can you run through that pain?
- Who can you call on for help so you can finish the race?

experiencing

Meditate and pray this week about determination in your life and ministry...

Lord, I know you're cheering me on. When my legs are weary and my breathing labored, you lift and carry me. Help me to rest in your care so I can run the best race possible. Amen.

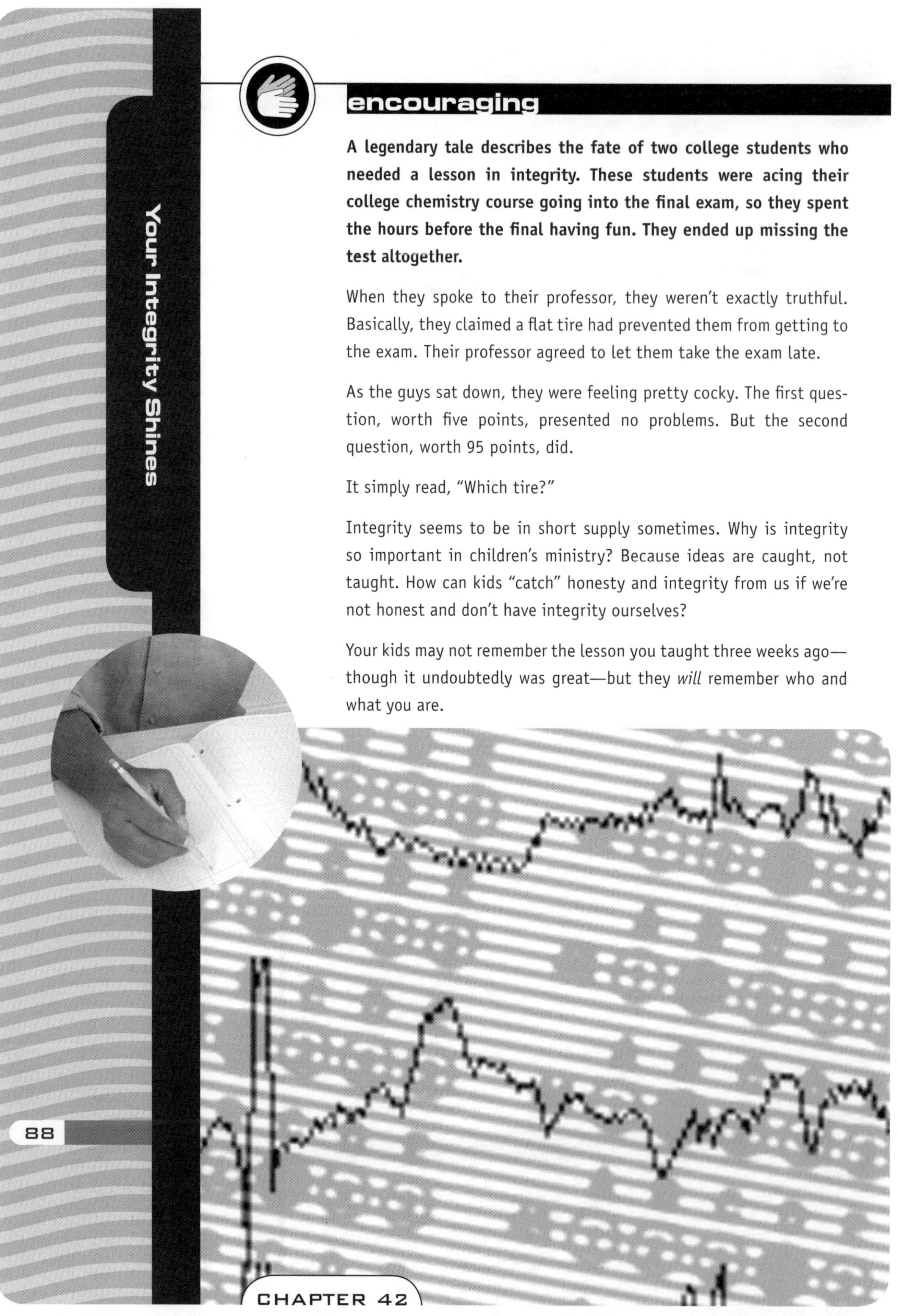

encouraging

A legendary tale describes the fate of two college students who needed a lesson in integrity. These students were acing their college chemistry course going into the final exam, so they spent the hours before the final having fun. They ended up missing the test altogether.

When they spoke to their professor, they weren't exactly truthful. Basically, they claimed a flat tire had prevented them from getting to the exam. Their professor agreed to let them take the exam late.

As the guys sat down, they were feeling pretty cocky. The first question, worth five points, presented no problems. But the second question, worth 95 points, did.

It simply read, "Which tire?"

Integrity seems to be in short supply sometimes. Why is integrity so important in children's ministry? Because ideas are caught, not taught. How can kids "catch" honesty and integrity from us if we're not honest and don't have integrity ourselves?

Your kids may not remember the lesson you taught three weeks ago—though it undoubtedly was great—but they *will* remember who and what you are.

engaging

Write down a statement that expresses your personal commitment to living with integrity. Post it on your refrigerator or in your car so it will be a daily reminder.

empowering

"Blessed are those whose lives have integrity, those who follow the teachings of the Lord."

—Psalm 119:1 *(God's Word)*

equipping

Choosing a life of integrity means choosing, day in and day out, to do the right thing. The decisions aren't always easy or even clear, but the person with integrity works hard to choose wisely.

- What's an example of a way you've demonstrated integrity in your life?
- What area of your life could use a little "integrity housecleaning"?
- How can you help your kids "catch" integrity?

experiencing

Meditate and pray this week about integrity in your life and ministry...

Lord, you've shown us through your own life how to live with integrity. Thank you for your example. I know I'll face temptation in this world that accepts lies and questionable ethics from most of our "heroes." I'll keep my eyes on you, Lord. Thank you for showing me the way. Amen.

encouraging

Recently I was pulled over by my "friends" in the California Highway Patrol—for the third time. The first time they pulled me over, I was over-the-top nice and pleasant. I kept my hands on the steering wheel in full view so as not to concern the officer. I handed over my license, proof of insurance, and registration quickly and with poise. I answered the direct questions with direct responses. Bottom line—I still got a ticket. An expensive one, too.

The second time I was pulled over, I produced my documentation a little more slowly. I was cordial, but not overly friendly. I still got a ticket.

The third time, I said to the officer, "Here's my license, registration, and proof of insurance. I was wrong. I blew it. I'm in a hurry, so can you just do whatever you need to do quickly?"

Yep, I got the ticket—and the process took twice as long as before! At the end of our time together, the officer told me he'd been planning to issue me a warning, but my attitude had earned me the ticket.

A little cordial dialogue could have made a huge difference to my pocketbook...and my witness to the officer.

engaging

This week read James 3, and jot down a few ways what we say can make a difference. Commit to using your words carefully, as powerful tools for encouragement and empowerment.

empowering

"A wise, mature person is known for his understanding. The more pleasant his words, the more persuasive he is."

—Proverbs 16:21 *(TEV)*

equipping

Choosing the right words isn't always easy. But the blessings the effort sends to others, and returns to you, makes the effort worthwhile.

- How could using careful dialogue have made a positive difference in your life last week?
- How have you successfully approached a situation that required carefully chosen words in the past?
- How could a few carefully chosen words make a difference in the life of a co-teacher this week? a parent? a child? What might those words be?

experiencing

Meditate and pray this week about dialogue in your life and ministry...

Lord, your Word tells us what a strong tool the tongue is. Paul reminds us that we should be kind and pleasant when we answer people. Please help me to use words that heal, not words that hurt. Help me use words that build up, not words that tear down. Amen.

encouraging

There are two evenings each year my twins want to go to bed early: Christmas Eve and the eve of their birthday. As they climb into the car after school, they announce that they want to go right home and go to bed. When we remind them that it's three in the afternoon, they say, "We know. But we want tomorrow to hurry up and be here!"

Why do kids want to go to bed early before these special occasions? Because they're anticipating joy. Turning six doesn't exactly bring great advantages over being five. But turning six means gifts, cake, and parties—joy!

I'd love for us to experience our spiritual "birthdays" with the same anticipation and joy that kids experience their physical birthdays.

Do you remember when you invited Christ to reign supreme in your life? Do you celebrate that day by giving thanks to the one who paid for that gift of salvation?

Circle that date now on your calendar, and decide now to celebrate.

engaging

Reflect on your spiritual birthday. How did your decision to commit your life to Jesus affect your life? If you remember the day, mark it on your calendar as a day to celebrate. Take five minutes every day this week to thank God for that gift.

empowering

"You will receive your salvation with joy as you would draw water from a well. At that time you will say, 'Praise the Lord and worship him. Tell everyone what he has done and how great he is.' " —Isaiah 12:3-4 *(NCV)*

equipping

Isaiah 12:3-4 reminds us to receive joy as if we were drawing water from a well. Picture yourself walking for miles in the scorching, sunbaked desert. Drawing water would bring elation and joy!

- What does God's love *really* mean to you?

- How did you feel when you first experienced God's love?

- How can you cultivate that sense of joy regularly in your daily life?

experiencing

Meditate and pray this week about the joy of salvation in your life and ministry...

Lord, when I think about what you did for me on the cross, I'm humbled by your sacrifice. I'm horrified by your pain. I'm encouraged by your faith. I'm joyful about your love. Thank you, Lord! Thank you for making it possible for me to be a forgiven child of God. Amen.

encouraging

Shelia and Jack had dated for nearly two years, so going out on a Friday night to catch a movie was no big deal. But *this* date could be the Big One, Shelia thought—the night Jack would propose. Jack said they'd be going someplace special, so Shelia spent more money than she thought possible on a dress. She primped. She powdered. And when Shelia answered her door that night, she took Jack's breath away.

The restaurant was flawless. The ride in the carriage was a dream. And when Jack turned to Sheila, she felt her heart nearly stop beating.

"I've been wanting to ask you something all night," he said nervously. "I was wondering...I mean...I was *hoping*...would you mind if we headed back so I could catch the rest of the playoff game?"

There's a point here: Sometimes we get so caught up in the package that we miss the heart of what's inside. Maybe Jack can pull off a great date, but—news flash to Shelia—that's the package. Inside, he'll probably always be the kind of guy who wants to watch the playoffs.

In ministry we can get caught up in the package too. We like the church, enjoy the kids, appreciate the kudos that come our way because we teach. But what's *important* is the heart of the matter: that we're serving God and loving kids. The rest is just packaging.

What matters most is our connecting with kids, and connecting those kids to God. The rest is packaging.

How are you doing with helping those connections happen? And do you want to do even better?

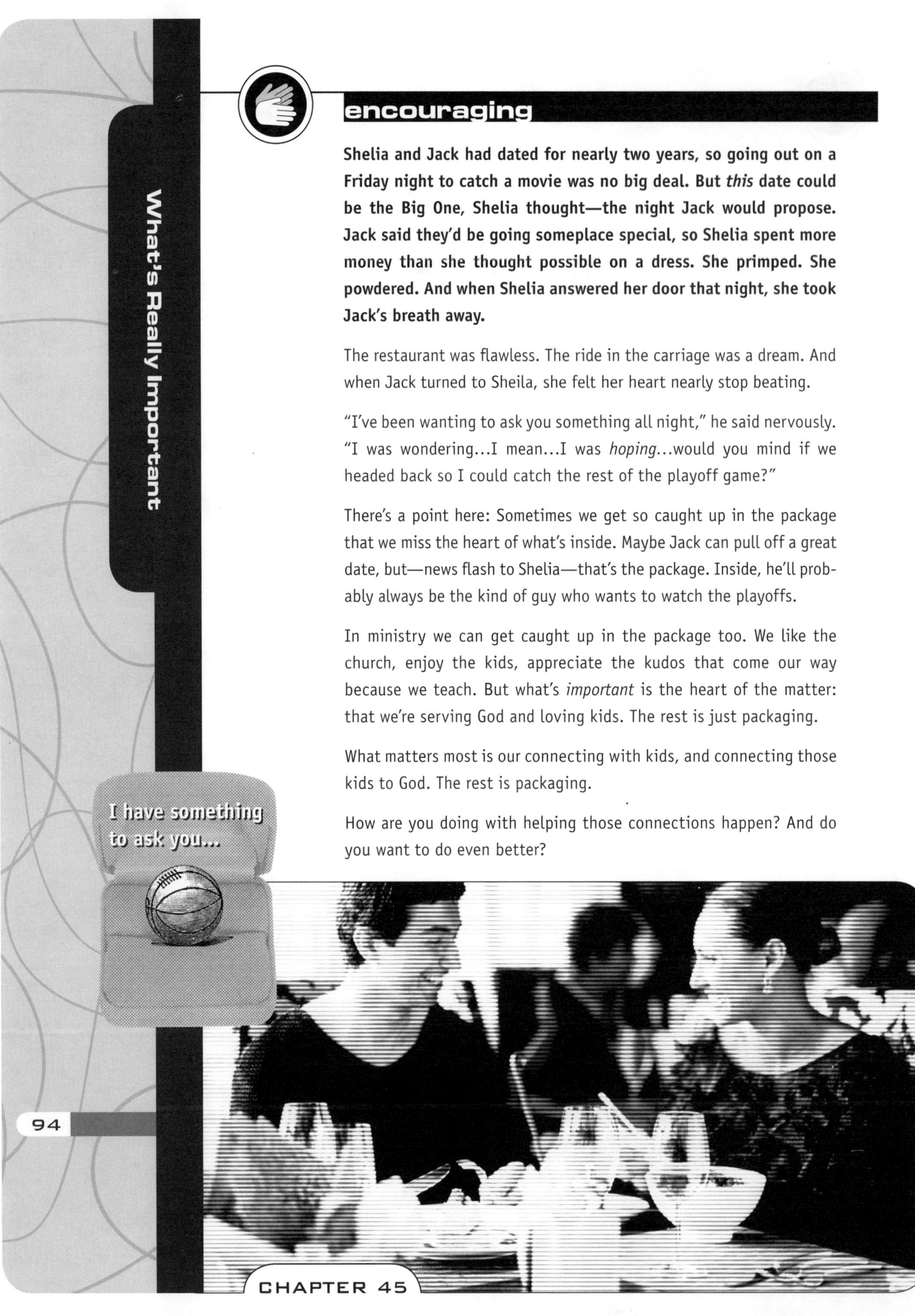

engaging

This week, make a list of a few things that distract you from connecting to kids in your ministry area. With a fellow teacher, review the list. What can you do to fix what you've listed so you can focus on the kids?

empowering

"Then the people brought their little children to Jesus so he could put his hands on them and pray for them. His followers told them to stop, but Jesus said, 'Let the little children come to me. Don't stop them, because the kingdom of heaven belongs to people who are like these children.'" —Matthew 19:13-14 *(NCV)*

equipping

Focus is good, but we want to make sure we're focusing on the right things—the person instead of the playoffs.

- How would you describe what's really important in your personal life?
- How would you describe what's really important in your ministry?
- How can you safeguard your focus on those things?

experiencing

Meditate and pray this week about what's really important in your life and ministry...

Lord, thank you for the children who come to our church. Please watch over these children and their specific needs...And help me welcome children as Jesus did, instead of allowing less important details to distract me. Keep me focused on one thing—helping kids develop a growing relationship with you. Amen.

encouraging

When John F. Kennedy visited San Antonio during his 1960 campaign, a prominent local citizen gave the presidential candidate a tour of the Alamo. As the crowds outside pressed closer, Kennedy grew uneasy. "Get me out the back door," he reportedly said. "I've got a plane to catch."

Kennedy's host, Maury Maverick Jr., replied, "There is no back door. That's why they were all heroes."

I'll be honest with you. Sometimes I want to give up and quit. Show me the back door! But when difficult times enter our lives, God can use them to make us better leaders and Christ-followers.

There are no back doors to our relationships, our ministries, our jobs, our calling, or our kids. We *will* reap a harvest—not one blessing, but a harvest of blessings—if we don't give up.

engaging

This week, every time you see an "exit" sign, repeat to yourself, "There are no back doors, so I'm going to face life and be a hero!"

empowering

"So let's not allow ourselves to get fatigued doing good. At the right time we will harvest a good crop if we don't give up, or quit."

—Galatians 6:9 *(The Message)*

equipping

I've seen many people escape difficult situations by walking out the back door. What they don't see is that the situations often walk out right behind them. Hang in there. Don't give up. Blessings will follow.

- What situations are you facing right now for which you'd really like a back door?

- Why do you want a back door?

- What might you do in response to those situations besides look for a back door?

experiencing

Meditate and pray this week about back doors in your life and ministry...

Lord, I'm facing some really tough situations right now, and I'm tempted to run out the back door. Strengthen me with your courage and persistence so I can confront situations that feel frightening or overwhelming. Build my character and my leadership through these trials. Thank you for your comfort, wisdom, and strength. I know we're in this together. Amen.

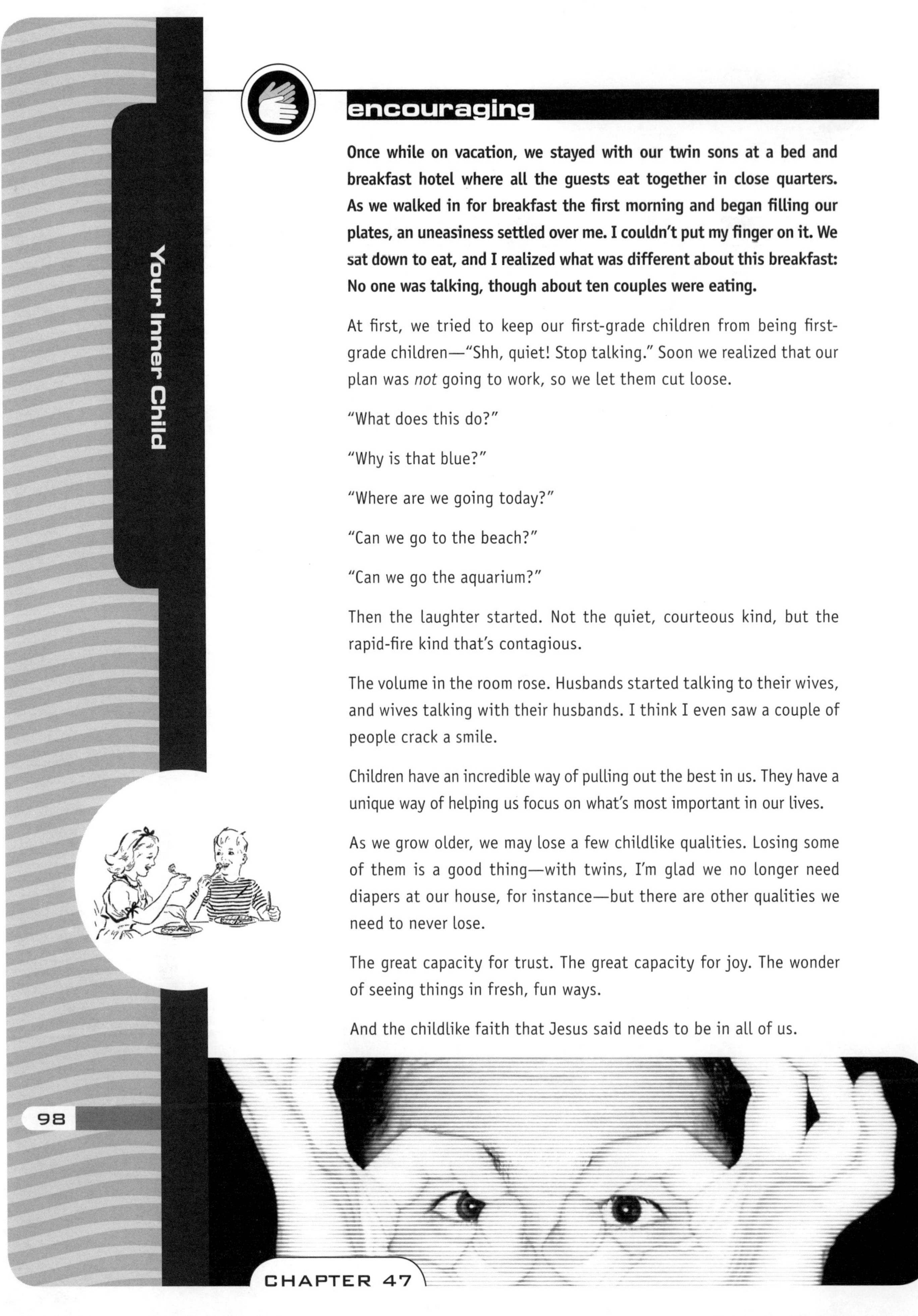

encouraging

Once while on vacation, we stayed with our twin sons at a bed and breakfast hotel where all the guests eat together in close quarters. As we walked in for breakfast the first morning and began filling our plates, an uneasiness settled over me. I couldn't put my finger on it. We sat down to eat, and I realized what was different about this breakfast: No one was talking, though about ten couples were eating.

At first, we tried to keep our first-grade children from being first-grade children—"Shh, quiet! Stop talking." Soon we realized that our plan was *not* going to work, so we let them cut loose.

"What does this do?"

"Why is that blue?"

"Where are we going today?"

"Can we go to the beach?"

"Can we go the aquarium?"

Then the laughter started. Not the quiet, courteous kind, but the rapid-fire kind that's contagious.

The volume in the room rose. Husbands started talking to their wives, and wives talking with their husbands. I think I even saw a couple of people crack a smile.

Children have an incredible way of pulling out the best in us. They have a unique way of helping us focus on what's most important in our lives.

As we grow older, we may lose a few childlike qualities. Losing some of them is a good thing—with twins, I'm glad we no longer need diapers at our house, for instance—but there are other qualities we need to never lose.

The great capacity for trust. The great capacity for joy. The wonder of seeing things in fresh, fun ways.

And the childlike faith that Jesus said needs to be in all of us.

engaging

Take a moment to list three or four childlike qualities you need to recapture. Then ask: What might nurture the child within me and help me engage life—and ministry—with enthusiasm?

empowering

"But Jesus called for the children, saying, 'Let the little children come to me. Don't stop them, because the kingdom of God belongs to people who are like these children.' "

—Luke 18:16 *(NCV)*

equipping

Nurture your "inner child"! It's a matter of learning more about your Lord's kingdom.

- What do you think Christ was talking about when he said the kingdom of God belongs to people who are childlike?
- How do you help bring out childlike qualities in others?
- How can you encourage your own childlike qualities to shine?

experiencing

Meditate and pray this week about being childlike in your life and ministry...

Lord, you embraced children not only for their intrinsic worth, but also for the way they exemplify faith and hope. Help me to grow these childlike attributes in my own life...I am privileged to work with these little ambassadors. Thank you for the children and what they teach me. Amen.

encouraging

Ever had a rotten day at work? Keith Sanderson sure has. While operating some industrial chopping equipment for his job at Macy Panel Products in England, Sanderson chopped off part of his thumb.

Wait. It gets worse.

Sanderson had to explain to his manager what had happened to his thumb, so he demonstrated with his other hand. That's when he chopped off his finger.

Sanderson's day went from bad to worse!

I'm sure some of your life experiences have taken you from bad to worse. Physically, emotionally, and socially, you've been cut—or you've cut someone else. Whether you're doing the slicing, or you're being sliced, there's pain. And a need for healing.

The good news is God is powerful, and there's no wound God can't heal.

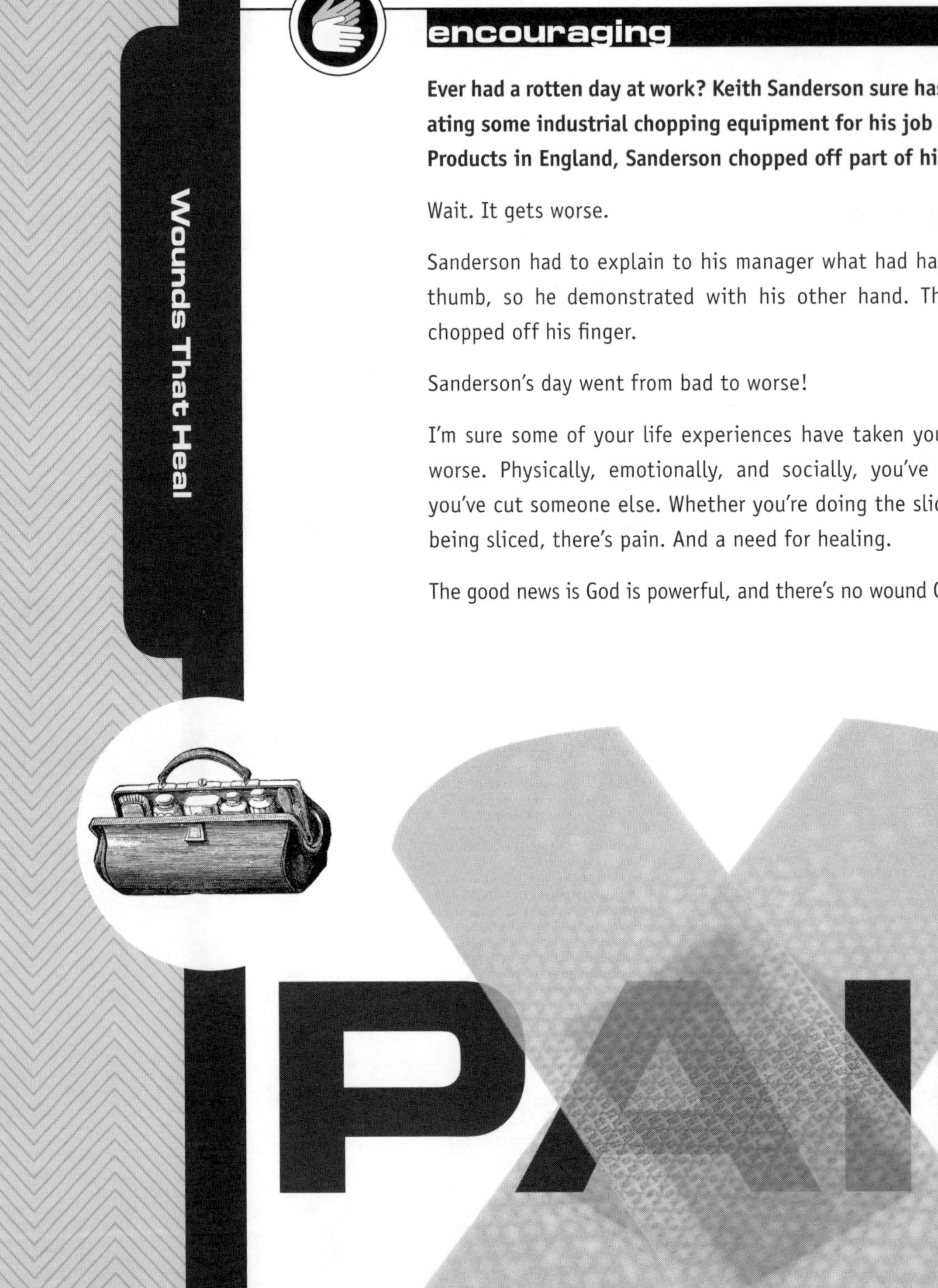

engaging

Take a moment now to list one or two ways you've felt cut this past week. Pray for God to completely heal each cut, and think about what you can do to help that process.

empowering

"People can never predict when hard times might come. Like fish in a net or birds in a snare, people are often caught by sudden tragedy."

—Ecclesiastes 9:12 *(NLT)*

equipping

I know people who suffered pain but who can now look back on the experience with a chuckle. We may recall the cuts, but the pain is gone because our Master Physician sympathizes and heals. God takes us from worse to bad to good to great.

- What wounds have you suffered in life that you can laugh about now?
- How do you think that was able to happen?
- Are there steps you can take, with God's help, to begin healing a fresh cut in your life?

experiencing

Meditate and pray this week about cuts in your life and ministry...

Lord, no one has suffered more than you. Your intimate understanding of my pain soothes the sting. These are the cuts I've received that need healing...These are cuts I've given to others that need healing...Thank you, Lord, for your healing touch. Amen.

encouraging

My wife and I joined friends one evening for dinner at a special-occasion, reservations-only restaurant. The restaurant is known for its exceptional food, exceptional service, and exceptional surroundings. We found another aspect to be exceptional too: the greetings.

From the time we came in to the time we were seated—about forty-five seconds—no fewer than seven people greeted us. On that short walk, the hostess, three servers, two bus boys, and the manager each said, "Hi! Welcome to our restaurant. We hope you enjoy your evening." I couldn't tell which staff member was having a bad day or whose car didn't work or who was having financial problems or who was tired. With cheerful enthusiasm, all seven of them smiled and welcomed us.

What do people remember about your church after they leave? What would happen if each child and parent who walked into your ministry area heard from the teachers, volunteers, and staff, "Hi! Welcome to our church. We hope you and your child enjoy the service"?

All restaurants serve is food and entertainment. We've got something more important to share. Let's share it in an exceptional way.

engaging

Discuss with your fellow teachers how *you* can welcome everyone who crosses your path. Write down what you'll say to the parents and children you greet.

empowering

"When you talk, you should always be kind and pleasant so you will be able to answer everyone in the way you should."

—Colossians 4:6 *(NCV)*

equipping

Smiling, happy, passionate people serving with each other and serving the Lord—what a great vision for parents and children to witness.

- When have you been enveloped by a warm, welcoming greeting? What was it like?

- What traits of Christ's are reflected through such a greeting?

- Who besides parents and kids needs an encouraging greeting from you?

experiencing

Meditate and pray this week about greeting others as you do life and ministry...

Lord, you welcome us with open arms. Give me those arms, too, so that I may share your welcome with others. Please provide energy and quickness of mind so that I can extend your loving greeting to each person I meet. Amen.

encouraging

One Saturday, I took my sons, Alec and Cameron, to the driving range. As we stood next to each other, hitting golf balls, Cameron suddenly stopped. "Dad, look at that," he said as he pointed into the sky.

Alec, in midswing, stopped and said, "Ooh, cool." A huge hawk circled in the blue sky.

"What are those little birds trying to do to that hawk?" my kids asked. Several small birds flew at the hawk, trying to scare it away.

The hawk continued to circle, unimpressed by their efforts. With purpose and resolve, the hawk refused distraction. A few minutes later, some of the little birds left. The rest did so when another hawk joined the first, circling in unison.

During the entire flight, the first hawk remained focused and soon had a companion by its side. In the same way, God wants us to stay focused, and he's our constant companion.

What "little birds" are threatening your focus this week?

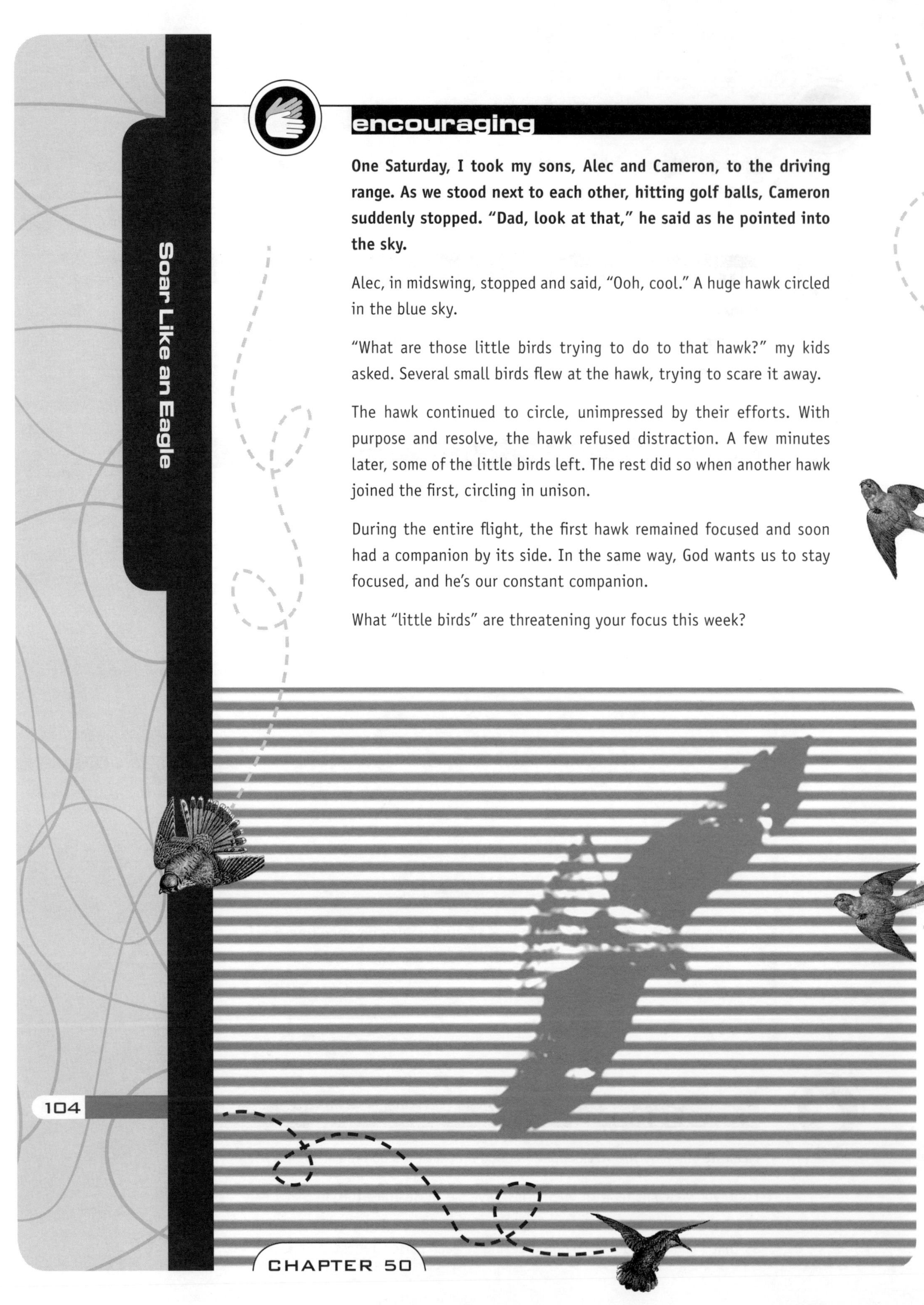

engaging

What "little birds" are threatening your focus this week? Confide in a friend what distractions you're struggling with, and ask him or her to call you midweek with encouragement to keep flying.

empowering

"But the people who trust the Lord will become strong again. They will rise up as an eagle in the sky; they will run and not need rest; they will walk and not become tired."

—Isaiah 40:31 *(NCV)*

equipping

The hawk was larger and probably could have knocked those little birds out of the sky. But he didn't sway. Calling, purpose, and laserlike focus can direct us in a similar way.

- What do you really need to persist with this week?

- What are your top strategies for dealing with distractions?

- What words motivate you to persist despite difficulties?

experiencing

Meditate and pray this week about persistence in your life and ministry...

Lord, my focus belongs to you. You are good. You are love. You are power. You are grace. You are my constant companion. As I rest in your care, the details and distractions fly away, and I soar on your eagle wings. Amen.

encouraging

During a layover at an airport, I stood in a long line at a well-known fast-food restaurant. I waited in line for about fifteen minutes, then placed my order with a very nice employee who was doing his best to manage the line that was quickly forming behind me. As I waited for my food, I counted: *Sixteen people* stood in line.

One employee worked the counter. One prepared the food. Three—yes, three—stood within five feet of me enjoying beverages. The backs of their restaurant-issued T-shirts read, "I'm making it happen!" A sign on the counter read, "Team service to serve you better."

What? This was laugh-out-loud funny! These employees' actions were *not* supporting the mission of the restaurant.

If we're not careful, even in children's ministry we can fall into the rut of just going through the motions. Just showing up and putting in our time.

Here's a question for you: If you were wearing a T-shirt with the mission statement of your children's ministry printed on it, would your actions match up?

engaging

Think about one area in your life or ministry where you feel you're not living fully. Then write down what you can do this week to get out of that rut and "make it happen!"

empowering

"Make sure you don't take things for granted and go slack in working for the common good; share what you have with others. God takes particular pleasure in acts of worship—a different kind of 'sacrifice'—that take place in kitchen and workplace and on the streets."

—Hebrews 13:16 *(The Message)*

equipping

When our actions contradict our mission, we lose impact. But with the help of the Holy Spirit, we can do amazing things in our lives and in the lives of others.

- What is God calling you to do?
- How can you begin to make that happen?
- Who can you enlist as encouragers to help keep your actions in line with your mission?

experiencing

Meditate and pray this week about making it happen in your life and ministry...

Lord, thank you for your guidance, for your call. This is an area of my life in which I feel the Holy Spirit is helping me to make it happen...Thank you for this work in my life. Please continue to give me courage, wisdom, and discernment in this area. Amen.

encouraging

Game 7 of the Stanley Cup Finals in hockey—there's nothing like it...at least for hockey fans like me. It's the end of a grueling season, the game that determines the "world champions." One team goes home with a trophy, and the other team just goes home.

Players can view Game 7 as an end or as a beginning. Those who view it as an end are correct. Win or lose, it's the end of the season.

Players who view it as a beginning are *also* correct. Win or lose, it's valuable experience players can carry forward into future seasons. At a time when most teams have already hung up their skates for the season, players in Game 7 are getting a head start on the coming year.

Going to work, raising a family, or leading a group of children at church can all be bumpy rides. We face ups and downs along the way.

Some people view the tough times in children's ministry as an end. They walk out of class grumbling, "I'll never teach fifth-graders again—I'm tired of being taped to the wall every week!"

Others view tough times in children's ministry as a beginning. When an activity falls flat, they start over the next week with something new.

Maybe you're experiencing a "game seven" challenge right now in your ministry. Whatever happened, ask the Lord for help and wisdom to learn from the experience. And consider the possibility that God may be using the tough time you're facing to refine your character in some way as he prepares to send you into next season.

engaging

Maybe you're experiencing a tough "game seven" right now. Ask the Lord for help and wisdom to navigate the trying circumstances. Ask God if he's trying to refine you somehow as a result of the tough times.

empowering

"Of course, my friends, I really do not think that I have already won it; the one thing I do, however, is to forget what is behind me and do my best to reach what is ahead."—Philippians. 3:13 *(TEV)*

equipping

Paul says to forget the past and reach forward. Every time we "fail" in ministry, we learn. Winners are empowered to learn from the past and apply them to new experiences. So one season may be ending, but another one is just ahead.

- What are some of those experiences through which you've felt like you've lost a "game seven"?
- What have you learned from those losses?
- How have those losses contributed to new beginnings?

experiencing

Meditate and pray this week about losses in your life and ministry...

Lord, you know how hard I try to serve you and the kids well. But sometimes I feel like I've just lost the big game. During those defeating times, please pick me up and put me back on my feet. Help me remember that a loss is really an opportunity to learn. Speak to me so that, with your help, a loss is transformed into a new, improved season. Amen.

Bonus Encouragement Posters!

Tacked on a bulletin board, slid into your teachers' in-boxes, tucked into an envelope along with a newsletter…these mini-posters are encouragers that take almost no time to create—and that have a huge impact.

Simply photocopy as many of these as you need for your church's children's workers and distribute them. They're words of encouragement from the most powerful source of encouragement of all: God's Word.

"Glory belongs to God, whose power is at work in us. By this power he can do infinitely more than we can ask or imagine."

—Ephesians 3:20 *(God's Word)*

You're not in ministry alone

or moving ahead under your own power.

God is with you!

"Then make me truly happy by agreeing wholeheart-edly with each other, loving one another, and working together with one heart and purpose."

—Philippians 2:2 *(NLT)*

We're a team!
Let's work together
to help kids know,
love, and follow Jesus!

"Be sure that you live in a way that brings honor to the Good News of Christ. Then whether I come and visit you or am away from you, I will hear good things about you. I will hear that you continue strong with one purpose and that you work together as a team for the faith of the Good News."

—Philippians 1:27 *(ICB)*

The most lasting lessons are caught, not taught. Let's live lives of integrity so the more kids know about us, the more they discover we love God.

"Dear brothers and sisters, whenever trouble comes your way, let it be an opportunity for joy."

—James 1:2 *(NLT)*

Having a tough day? Share it with someone on the ministry team so we can pray for you. And let's find joy in your journey!

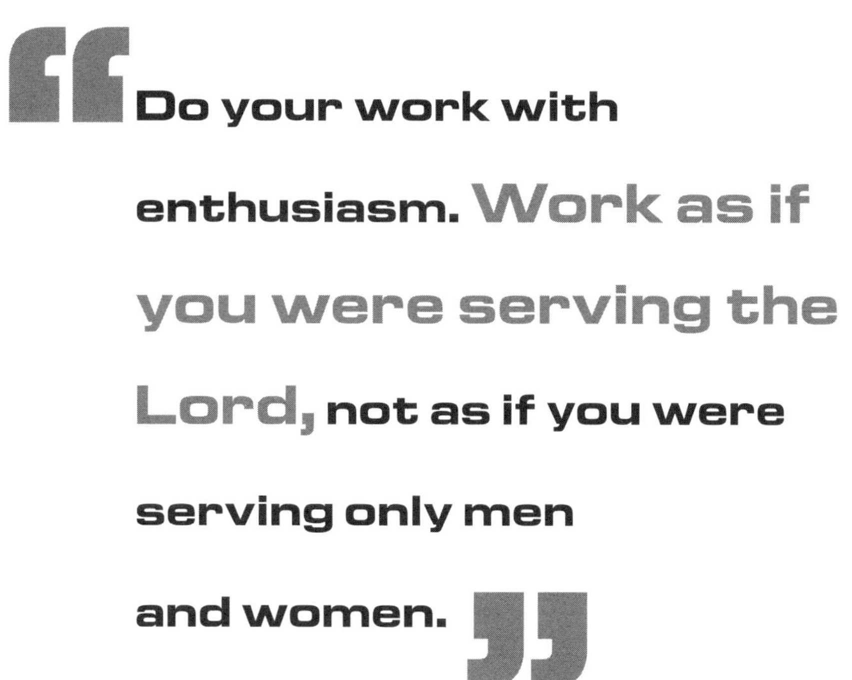

—Ephesians 6:7 *(NCV)*

You're not just teaching a lesson, *changing a diaper, or serving snacks; you're serving God! Thanks for being a faithful servant!*

Serve

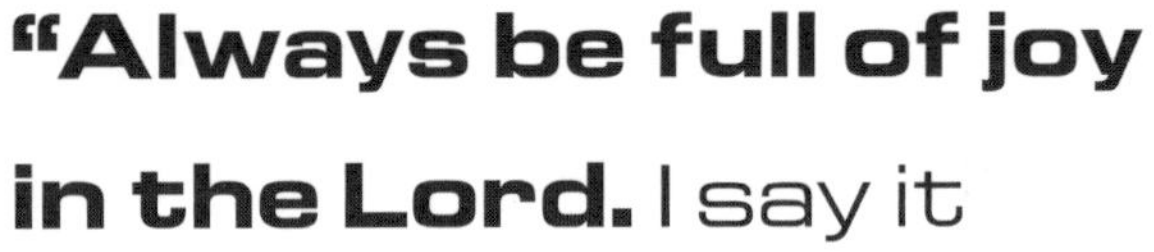

"Always be full of joy in the Lord. I say it again—rejoice!"

—Philippians 4:4 *(NLT)*

You have something to smile about! Let's share that joy with children in our ministry!

rejoice

"For I am convinced that neither death nor life, neither angels nor demons, neither the present nor the future, nor any powers, neither height nor depth, nor anything else in all creation, will be able to separate us from the love of God that is in Christ Jesus our Lord."

—Romans 8:38-39 *(NIV)*

What a promise! God knows and loves you with a love that's deep, wide, and eternal. Share that love with children!

"But those who wait upon God get fresh strength. They spread their wings and soar like eagles, they run and don't get tired, they walk and don't lag behind."

—Isaiah 40:31 *(The Message)*

There's a power far beyond your own *that will sustain you in ministry. Look to God for strength today!*

"Then God will strengthen you with his own great power. And you will not give up when troubles come, but you will be patient."

—Colossians 1:11 *(ICB)*

What troubles you today? Ask God for strength—and share your struggle with a team member who can pray for you!

strength

"Give all your worries and cares to God, for he cares about what happens to you."

—1 Peter 5:7 *(NLT)*

Wow! What a promise! You're not alone;

you're loved by God!

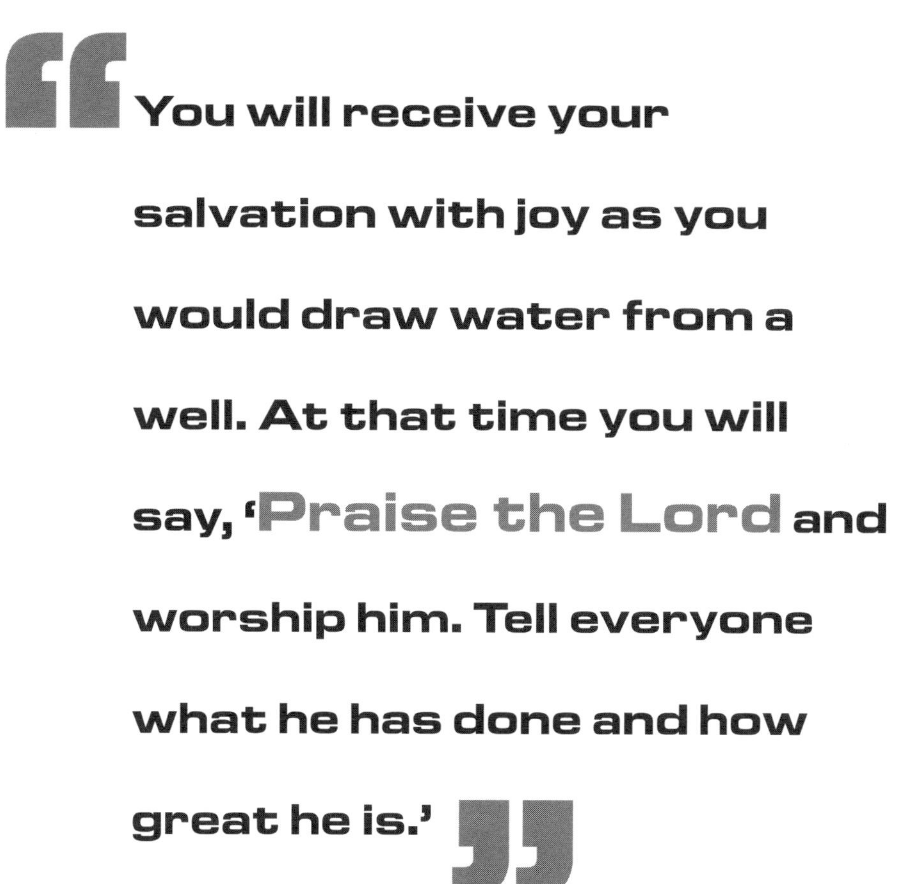

—Isaiah 12:3-4 *(NCV)*

When you're serving kids in children's ministry, you're doing what Isaiah prophesied. *What a privilege!*

Salvation

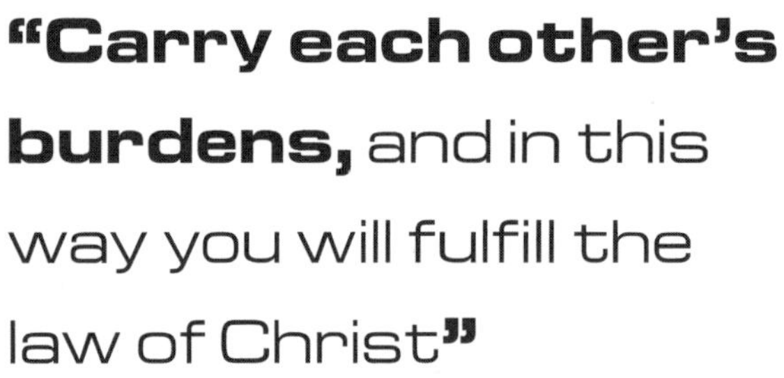

—Galatians 6:2 (NIV)

Let's be there for each other. How can you encourage another children's worker today?

"So let's not allow ourselves to get fatigued doing good. At the right time we will harvest a good crop if we don't give up, or quit."

—Galatians 6:9 *(The Message)*

You're planting good seed. The harvest will come in time. Don't grow tired of being a Christlike influence in the lives of children!

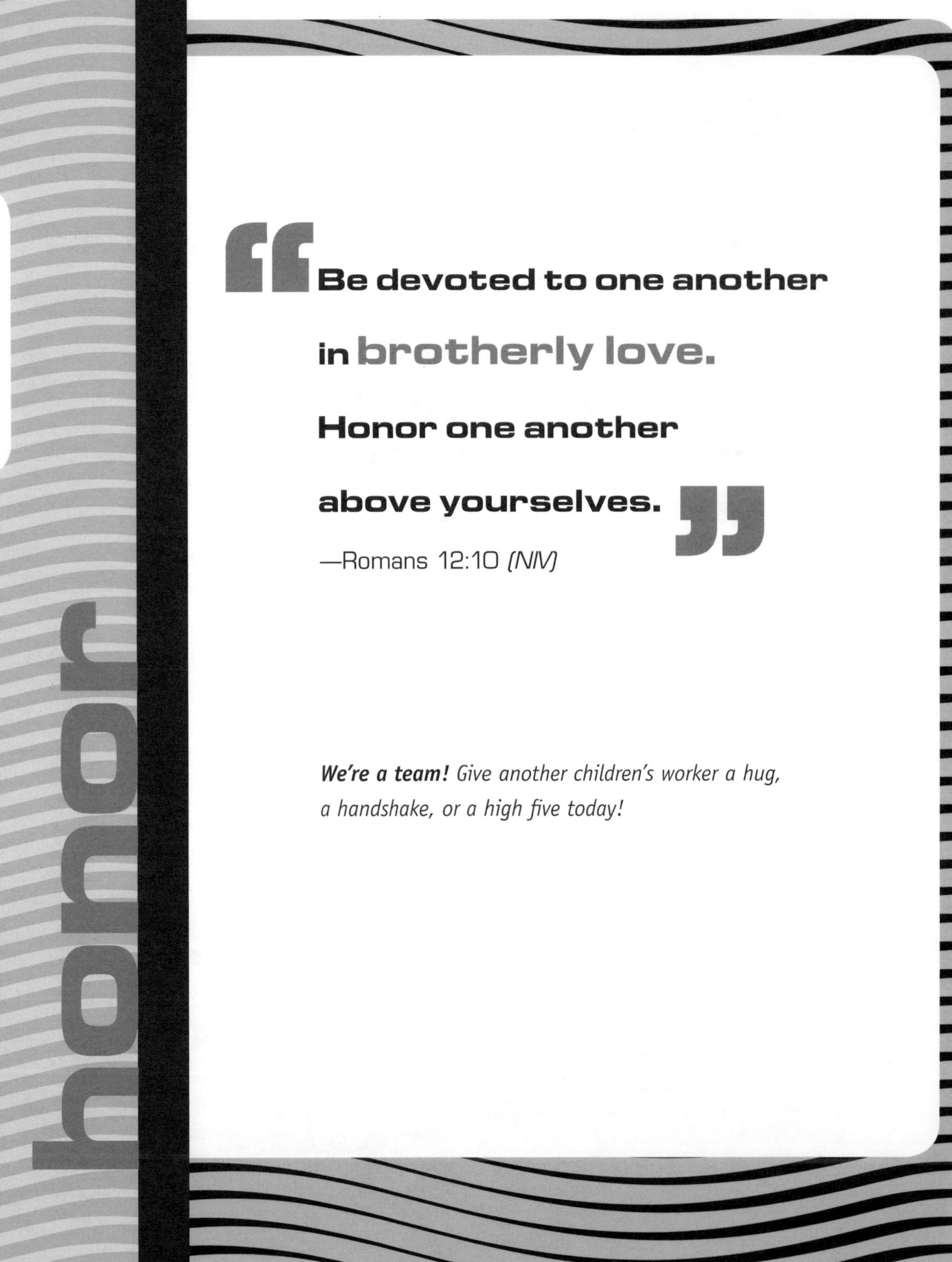

"Be devoted to one another in brotherly love. Honor one another above yourselves."

—Romans 12:10 *(NIV)*

We're a team! *Give another children's worker a hug, a handshake, or a high five today!*

"I have commanded you, 'Be strong and courageous! Don't tremble or be terrified, because the Lord your God is with you wherever you go.' "

—Joshua 1:9 *(God's Word)*

Onto the battlefield, into the classroom...you're not alone! Ask God to guide you and walk with you in your ministry to kids.

strong

"I am still not all I should be, but I am bringing all my energies to bear on this one thing: Forgetting the past and looking forward to what lies ahead, I strain to reach the end of the race and receive the prize for which God is calling us up to heaven because of what Christ Jesus did for us."

—Philippians 3:13-14 *(TLB)*

Everyone has a bad day now and then. Don't be discouraged—you have a glorious future! Invite as many children as possible to join you there!

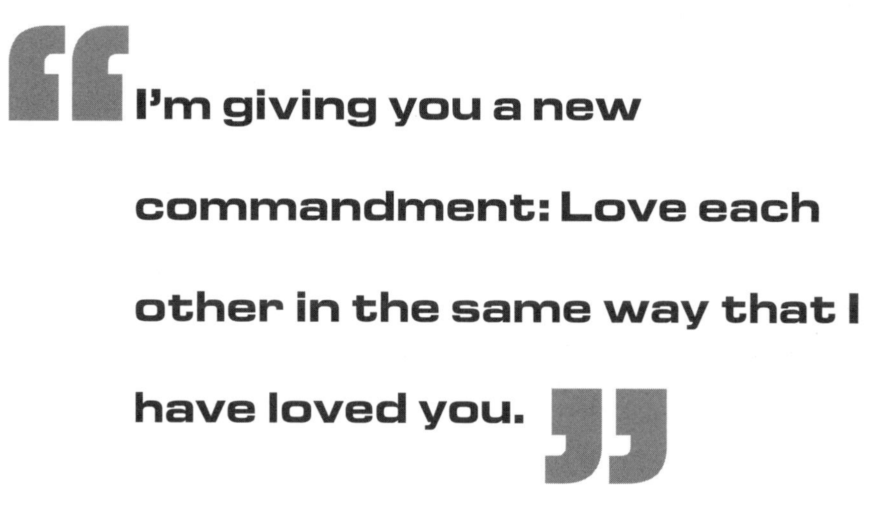

"I'm giving you a new commandment: Love each other in the same way that I have loved you."

—John 13:34 *(God's Word)*

When we honor and support each other, we show children how God's love looks when it's wearing skin. *Your loving attitude makes a difference!*

love